PLANT BASED DIET FOR BEGINNERS 2021

Plant-Based Diet Cookbook with 75 Delicious, Healthy Whole-Food Recipes

Copyright © 2021

No part of this publication may be reproduced, stored in a retrieval system, or transmitted in any form or by any means, electronic, mechanical, photocopying, recording, scanning, or otherwise

Limit of Liability/Disclaimer of Warranty: The Publisher and the author make no representations or warranties with respect to the accuracy or completeness of the contents of this work and specifically disclaim all warranties, including without limitation warranties of fitness for a particular purpose. No warranty may be created or extended by sales or promotional materials. The advice and strategies contained herein may not be suitable for every situation. This work is sold with the understanding that the Publisher is not engaged in rendering medical, legal, or other professional advice or services. If professional assistance is required, the services of a competent professional person should be sought. Neither the Publisher nor the author shall be liable for damages arising herefrom. The fact that an individual, organization, or website is referred to in this work as a citation and/or potential source of further information does not mean that the author or the Publisher endorses the information the individual, organization, or website may provide or recommendations they/it may make. Further, readers should be aware that websites listed in this work may have changed or disappeared between when this work was written and when it is read.

contents

INTRODUCTION

PART ONE: GETTING STARTED

CHAPTER 1
Why Go Plant-Based?

CHAPTER 2
Shopping List and Sample Menu

PART TWO: THE RECIPES

CHAPTER 3
Breakfasts
Whole-Wheat Blueberry Muffins
Walnut Crunch Banana Bread
Plant-Powered Pancakes
Maple-Pecan Granola
Paradise Island Overnight Oatmeal
Pumpkin Pie Oatmeal
Chocolate and Peanut Butter Quinoa
A.M. Breakfast Scramble
Loaded Breakfast Burrito
Southwest Sweet Potato Skillet

CHAPTER 4
Soups, Salads, and Sides

Lime-Mint Soup
Savory Split Pea Soup
Kale and Lentil Stew
Four-Can Chili
Vegan "Toona" Salad
Lemony Kale Salad
Southwest Spinach Salad
Asian-Style Slaw with Maple-Ginger Dressing
Whole-Wheat Pita Pockets
Creamy Potato Salad
Sautéed Collard Greens
Crispy Cauliflower Wings
Baked Taquitos with Fat-Free Refried Beans
15-Minute French Fries
Fluffy Mashed Potatoes with Gravy

CHAPTER 5
Entrées

BBQ Jackfruit Sliders
Hawaiian Luau Burgers
Falafel Burgers
Easy Vegan Pizza Bread
Baked Mac and Peas
Savory Sweet Potato Casserole
BBQ Tofu and Mashed Potato Bowl
Sunday Slow Roast
Oil-Free Rice-and-Vegetable Stir-Fry
Vegetable Spring Rolls with Spicy Peanut Dipping Sauce
Orange-Glazed Tofu Bowl
Mango-Ginger Chickpea Curry

Italian Bean Balls
Crispy Rice-and-Bean Tostadas
Southwest Stuffed Peppers
Easy Enchilada Bake
Burrito Bowl with Oil-Free Tortilla Chips
Homestyle Lentil Loaf with Maple-Balsamic Glaze

CHAPTER 6
Smoothies and Beverages
Watermelon Limeade
Bubbly Orange Soda
Creamy Cashew Milk
Homemade Oat Milk
Lucky Mint Smoothie
Paradise Island Smoothie
Apple Pie Smoothie
Peanut Butter and Chia Smoothie
Lean Green Chocolate Smoothie
Lemon-Ginger Tea
Cold-Brew Peach Iced Tea
Maple-Cinnamon Latte

CHAPTER 7
Snacks and Desserts
Kale Chips
Showtime Popcorn
Strawberry-Avocado Toast with Balsamic Glaze
Strawberry-Watermelon Ice Pops
Chocolate-Peppermint Nice Cream
Peanut Butter Nice Cream
Sweet Potato Pie Nice Cream
Oat Crunch Apple Crisp
Sweet Potato Spice Cake

Chocolate Microwave Mug Cake

CHAPTER 8

Sauces, Dressings, and Dips

Sweet and Tangy Ketchup (with BBQ Sauce Option)

Easy One-Pot Vegan Marinara

Sunflower Parmesan "Cheese"

Anytime "Cheese" Sauce (with Queso Option)

Plant-Powered "Sour Cream" (with Ranch Option)

Strawberry-Peach Vinaigrette

Lemon and Poppy Seed Dressing

Roasted Garlic Dressing

Roasted Jalapeño and Lime Guacamole

White Bean and Chickpea Hummus

The Dirty Dozen™ and the Clean Fifteen™

Measurement Conversions

Resources

Introduction

Congratulations on taking the first steps on your plant-based journey! Whether you're completely new to this way of eating or already somewhat familiar with it, I hope you find similar benefits to those I and many others have experienced following a plant-based diet.

I was born and raised in the Midwest eating the standard American diet (SAD). A love of athletics eventually led me to playing college football for the University of Nebraska while majoring in livestock production. But a few years into college, my life took a new direction after a career-ending back injury left me physically limited and unable to exercise. I became 100 pounds overweight, which is what made finding a way to regain my health through dietary means so important.

Searching for hope, I began researching the many diets that promised healthy and sustainable weight loss. Initially, my experience as a student studying animal science led me toward the many diets built on minimizing carbohydrates and maximizing protein and fat from animal sources. Though I followed the strict protocols of these diets, I wasn't seeing any positive results. I was extremely frustrated to find that my health was, in fact, deteriorating.

After exhausting what seemed like all of my options, I stumbled upon what is known as a whole-food, plant-based diet. Although this way of eating was completely unknown to me, I was surprised to find that it was common in some of the longest-living and healthiest populations around the globe. With nothing to lose, I decided to jump right in—and almost immediately began to see and feel positive results. Not only did my weight begin to drop, but my digestion improved, my skin cleared up, and the inflammation in my joints began to dissipate, too.

There was, of course, a learning curve. It was a dramatic change from the types of food I was used to eating and preparing. But I found that a few simple alterations made the switch to a plant-based diet easy, sustainable, and enjoyable. Over the course of the following two years, I was able to lose 100 pounds and completely regain my health.

While losing weight was my original goal, I believe my greatest accomplishment has been encouraging and leading many of my family members and friends to regain their own health. Building on what I've learned by helping others transition to and thrive on a plant-based diet, I've compiled my favorite recipes, techniques, and habits in this book. I truly believe that anyone can improve their health and quality of life through a plant-based diet—including you!

Vegan "Toona" Salad

getting started

PART ONE

CHAPTER 1
Why Go Plant-Based?

It's my pleasure to welcome you not just to a diet but to a new lifestyle. As someone who was once in your shoes, I know that changing the way you eat can seem daunting. But keep in mind that this way of eating is not about what you can't eat; it's about all the delicious, nutritious foods you can eat. My goal with this book is to empower you to enjoy all the benefits of a whole-food, plant-based diet. So before we dive into the recipes, let's take a closer look at what exactly a whole-food, plant-based diet is and why it's so great.

What Is a Plant-Based Diet?

In recent years, the term "plant-based" has grown in popularity, but it still means different things to different people. Some think a plant-based diet consists mostly of plant foods but allows some animal products. Others consider it a vegan diet, consisting of "anything without a mother or a face." In this book, I would like to introduce you to a whole-food, plant-based diet, also known as a WFPB diet. Here, we define a plant-based diet as one built around plant foods that are minimally processed. It excludes animal products and limits the use of salt, oil, and sugar.

WHOLE FOODS

Whole foods are foods eaten in their natural state, or as close to it as possible. Some examples are fruits, vegetables, nuts, seeds, legumes (beans, peas, lentils), and whole grains (brown rice, quinoa, oats). Compared to diets that include highly processed foods, whole-food diets are lower in calories, higher in fiber, and more conducive to a healthy body weight. Research on the health effects of whole foods, including a 2009 study in *The American Journal of Clinical Nutrition* and a 2006 study in *Diabetes Care*, shows that they provide many advantages, including better health outcomes for those suffering from heart disease and diabetes.

PLANT-BASED FOODS

Plant-based foods are those that don't come from animal sources like meat, dairy, eggs, and seafood. You might also know them as "vegan." The WFPB diet allows all whole plant foods as well as some plant-based foods that may be slightly more processed, as long as they aren't highly refined and don't contain any added salt, oil, or sugar.

Many lightly processed plant-based foods can be used as healthy alternatives to commonly consumed animal-based foods, such as cashew milk instead of cow's milk, a tofu scramble (here) instead of scrambled eggs, and shredded jackfruit (here) instead of pulled pork. Some other great plant-based foods included in a WFPB diet are whole-grain pastas and breads, corn tortillas, and many homemade sauces, dressings, and dips (chapter 8).

It's important to note that a healthy WFPB diet is built around whole plant foods in addition to those slightly processed plant-based foods. Together, they help ensure that we can change our current health for the better and also improve our chances of living longer and more active lives.

> ### RELATED LIFESTYLES
>
> **While I consider a WFPB diet to be the healthiest option, others may approach eating a more plant-centered diet in a number of ways. These approaches focus on moving away from the standard American diet (SAD) and toward a more plant-centered way of eating. Below are a few of the common plant-centered diets and brief descriptions of what they consist of.**
>
> Vegan. People who adhere to a vegan diet abstain from eating any foods derived from animals or their use (e.g., meat, milk, eggs, fish, or honey).
>
> Vegetarian. Those following a vegetarian way of eating do not eat meat or fish but still consume animal products like milk, eggs, and honey.
>
> Pescatarian. Pescatarians eat a vegetarian diet with the addition of fish and other seafood.
>
> Flexitarian. Those who are flexitarian mainly eat a vegetarian diet, while occasionally consuming animal-based foods.

SOS: SALT, OIL, AND SUGAR

After addressing animal products, the next set of questions most people have about a whole-food, plant-based diet revolves around salt, oil, and sugar. The optimum state of a WFPB diet is "SOS-free": free of salt, oil, and sugar. This is where you'll find the greatest health benefits, and for that reason, all the recipes in this book are SOS-free. You'll probably find that the longer you follow a WFPB diet, the better you'll be able to taste your food's natural flavors, creating less of a need for salt and sugar. But while you're transitioning, any movement toward a more SOS-free diet is a step in the right direction, so don't feel bad if you don't want to quit them all at once. Let's take a look at why it's so important to minimize your consumption of salt, oil, and sugar.

Salt

In recent years, there has been a lot of debate about whether or not salt has a place in a healthy diet. For those with health conditions like cardiovascular disease or hypertension, a low- or no-salt diet is recommended. Healthy individuals may also look to lower their overall salt intake to avoid developing issues like these in the first place.

There are a few tips that can help in the transition to a low- or no-salt diet. The largest percentage of the average person's dietary salt intake can be found in processed or preserved foods like cured meats, cheeses, and packaged snack foods. Since these foods are not considered a part of a healthy WFPB diet, the simple act of eating less of them while eating more fresh whole foods will greatly reduce your salt intake. If you still want a little salt with your meals as you get started, try adding it only after your food has been cooked. This allows you to taste the salt and avoid overdoing it.

Oil

Of the three ingredients mentioned in a SOS-free diet, the exclusion of oil can produce the most benefits. A 2005 study in *The American Journal of Medicine* found that oil-free WFPB diets result in significant weight loss, even without limiting subjects' "portion size or energy intake." In a 2005 study in *Integrative Medicine,* Dr. Caldwell Esselstyn Jr.'s groundbreaking research showed that an oil-free WFPB diet reduced average total cholesterol "from 246 mg/dL to 132 mg/dL and resulted in an opening of clogged arteries in 70 percent of his patients."

When thinking about oil in your diet, you may be wondering whether some oils are healthier than others. In 2007, a study was conducted to determine the effects that olive, soybean, and palm oils had on healthy individuals. That study, published in *Nutrition, Metabolism & Cardiovascular Diseases*, found that any type of oil had an adverse effect on endothelial function and increased triglycerides. For these reasons, the recipes included in this book will all be oil-free.

HOW DO I COOK WITHOUT OIL?

For those recipes you already cook at home, there are some easy alternatives that can help the transition to oil-free cooking go smoothly.

- You can sauté on the stovetop using water or low-sodium vegetable broth instead of oil. Since water evaporates when heated, you may need to add a splash more as the vegetables cook to keep them from sticking.
- When baking, substitute a fruit purée or applesauce (for sweeter dishes) or a blended vegetable purée (for savory dishes) to keep your baked goods from drying out.
- When cooking in the oven, use a sheet of parchment paper or a silicone mat to line baking sheets. This will prevent food from sticking to the sheet, even without oil.

- There are also some high-quality nonstick cookware brands that may be a worthwhile investment. (See "The Plant-Based Kitchen".)

Sugar

Sugar has become a much-studied topic in regard to weight loss, obesity, and healthy living. Before explaining why sugar is excluded in a WFPB, SOS-free diet, we need to make the important distinction between highly refined sugars (like corn syrup or table sugar) and the sugar naturally contained in carbohydrate-rich plant foods like fruit, whole grains, and root vegetables. When sugar is consumed in its natural whole-plant form, it is combined with water, phytonutrients, and health-promoting fiber, which means your body handles it differently from refined sugar. A 2003 study in *The American Journal of Clinical Nutrition* found that regular consumption of fruits and vegetables naturally high in fiber is "associated with reduced risk of cancer, cardiovascular disease, stroke, Alzheimer disease, cataracts, and some of the functional declines associated with aging."

Refined sugars, on the other hand, have been shown to have severe adverse effects on health outcomes, including learning, memory, obesity, and cardiovascular health. In the recipes in this book, you'll notice that the only ingredients used for sweetness will be various fruits (such as dates, bananas, and orange juice) or pure maple syrup, which is a less processed alternative to highly refined sugars. (If you'd like to omit the maple syrup or substitute a fruit purée, the recipes will still turn out great.)

Why WFPB?

Eating a WFPB diet has many benefits, including promoting animal welfare, protecting the environment, and improving health. Let's take a closer look at the reasons someone might adopt a WFPB diet.

ANIMAL CRUELTY

One benefit of choosing to eat a WFPB diet is the impact it has on animals. In 2018, the USDA predicted the average American would eat 222 pounds of red meat and poultry, not including dairy, eggs, and fish. The majority of animals raised for food are subjected to incredibly inhumane practices, spending the majority of their short lives in tight "living" spaces where they have little or no room to move. This is the case with egg-laying hens in battery cages, female pigs in gestation crates, cows on feedlots, and fish stuffed into offshore cages.

It's not only animals raised specifically for meat that suffer this cruelty. Male chicks born on egg-laying farms, male calves born on dairies, hens whose egg production has declined, sheep with low wool weights, and dairy cows whose production has fallen below industry standards end up in the same slaughterhouses as their relatives raised specifically for meat. Keeping animals out of the kitchen and opting for a WFPB diet is one of the largest impacts you can have in terms of reducing animal cruelty.

> *Many people think that eating an exclusively animal-free diet is more expensive than a more omnivorous diet. In reality, many bulk staples like whole grains, legumes, fruits, and vegetables can be purchased for much less than many animal-based foods.*

ENVIRONMENTAL IMPACT

Another reason for eating a WFPB diet is the beneficial impact it has on the environment. As a 2014 study in *The American Journal of Clinical Nutrition* found, "plant-based diets in comparison to meat-based diets are more sustainable." According to the Food and Agriculture Organization (FAO) of the United Nations, animal agriculture is a leading greenhouse gas producer responsible for 18 percent of the world's greenhouse gas emissions. In fact, the FAO report *Livestock's Long Shadow* shows that the animal agriculture sector is responsible for more global greenhouse gas emissions than all the transportation sectors combined. One UK-based study published in 2014 in the journal *Climatic Change* found that people who completely omit animal-based products were responsible for less than half as much greenhouse gas emission as those consuming moderate amounts of animal products.

As we look at feeding a rapidly increasing world population, land use is becoming ever more important. According to the FAO, in 2006, livestock production accounted for 70 percent of all agricultural land use. A 2013 study in *Environmental Research Letters* found that "36 percent of the calories produced by the world's crops are being used for animal feed and as biofuel feedstocks," and if everyone made the switch to eating foods that are exclusively grown for direct human consumption, we could "increase available food calories by as much as 70 percent, which could feed an additional 4 billion people." This is all to say that by eating a WFPB diet, we all have the power to affect the environment for the better.

HEALTH

Personal health is one of the main reasons many people begin a whole-food, plant-based diet. One of the many diseases a WFPB diet has been shown to prevent, treat, or reverse is obesity. As of 2012, "the prevalence of obesity in the United States was 16.9 percent in youth and 34.9 percent in adults," according to the *Journal of the American Medical Association* . These statistics are even more alarming when we take into account that "overweight and obesity are associated with a number of chronic diseases, including type 2 diabetes, metabolic syndrome, hypertension, and cardiovascular disease." The good news is that research, such as a 2015 *Eating Behaviors* study, shows that individuals who begin eating more plant foods have greater results when it comes to weight loss.

A related problem, heart disease, is currently the number one killer among adults in the United States. This is a disease that increases in prevalence as individuals consume more animal-based foods and rely less on whole plant foods. Summarizing his groundbreaking research on heart disease in a *Journal of Geriatric Cardiology* study, Dr. Caldwell Esselstyn Jr. proclaimed that "WFPB can restore the ability of endothelial cells to produce nitric oxide, which can halt and reverse disease without morbidity, mortality, or added expense."

Long-term research has also shown how meatless diets affect diabetes. One 17-year study in *Annals of Nutrition & Metabolism* found that "weekly meat intake was associated with a 74 percent increase . . . in odds of diabetes relative to long-term adherence to a vegetarian diet (zero meat intake)." One team of doctors, publishing in Kaiser Permanente's *Permanente Journal* , concluded that "plant-based diets may offer an advantage over those that are not plant-based with respect to prevention and management of diabetes."

Beyond the treatment of the aforementioned chronic diseases, healthy individuals can also benefit greatly from a WFPB diet. Dan Buettner's research on "blue zones," where the world's longest-lived populations are located, has shown that one major common denominator among long-lived populations is eating a more plant-based diet. The Seventh-day Adventists of Loma Linda, California, are a blue-zone population that has been studied for decades through what are known as the Adventist Health Studies. Some groundbreaking findings from a study in *Archives of Internal Medicine* : Meat-eating Adventists were twice as likely to develop dementia as vegetarians, and vegetarian men and women lived nine and six years longer, respectively, than their non-vegetarian counterparts.

ALWAYS, SOMETIMES, NEVER

Here are a few examples of the "always" foods that make up the base of the WFPB diet, the "sometimes" foods that are best enjoyed in moderation, and the "never" foods that aren't part of the diet at all.

ALWAYS	SOMETIMES	NEVER
Whole foods eaten as close to their natural state as possible	**Plant-based foods higher in fat or sugar** Minimally processed plant-based foods	**Animal products** **Processed foods** Sugar, oil, and salt
Whole grains: Rice, oats, barley, quinoa, dried corn Fruits: Apples, bananas, citrus, berries, melons, stone fruit Vegetables: Leafy greens (kale, lettuce, spinach, arugula, chard), broccoli, cauliflower, tomatoes, peppers, celery, green beans Starchy vegetables: Potatoes, sweet potatoes, carrots, beets Legumes: Beans, peas, lentils Mushrooms: Portobello, shiitake,	High-fat plant foods: Nuts, seeds, avocados Lightly processed foods: Whole-grain bread, whole-grain pasta, tofu Unsweetened plant-based milks: Soy milk, almond milk, cashew milk, oat milk, rice milk Sweeteners: Maple syrup, date paste, molasses	Meat: Beef, pork, chicken, lamb, venison, buffalo Seafood: Fish, shellfish, mollusks Dairy: Milk, butter, ghee, cheese, ice cream, whey Eggs Oils: Olive oil, sesame oil, canola oil, palm oil, peanut oil, coconut oil Processed vegan foods: Processed meat alternatives, packaged snacks, vegan ice cream Added sugar Added salt

oyster, chanterelle, porcini

Aromatics: Herbs and spices, onion, garlic, ginger, turmeric

Nutrition

Consuming a variety of foods on a WFPB diet is a healthy and delicious way to get your body all the nutrients it needs. You may have grown up being told the key to a healthy diet is to decrease carbohydrate intake and increase protein —but we'll soon look into why many plant-based physicians recommend the exact opposite. And while we will dive deeper into just how you can meet your macronutrient (carbohydrate, protein, fat) needs, the key thing to remember is to keep it simple and focus on eating whole plant foods, as close to their natural state as possible.

PROTEIN

People who have adopted a WFPB diet are often asked where they get their protein. This is based on the common misconception that protein is either only found in animal products or that protein from animal sources is of a higher quality than plant proteins. In reality, whole plant foods supply protein in various amounts, and a 2016 investigation in *JAMA Internal Medicine* shows that eating plant proteins is associated with lower rates of mortality, while those getting their protein from animal sources have higher risks of cardiovascular-related deaths. Another protein myth is that you need to eat specific "protein-rich" plant foods or supplements to meet your requirements on a WFPB diet. The truth is that by eating a well-rounded WFPB diet, you can rest assured knowing your protein needs are being met.

CARBOHYDRATES

Many popular diets require dieters to reduce or exclude carbohydrates. In contrast, a WFPB diet is built around carbohydrate-rich starchy staples, such as potatoes, sweet potatoes, oats, rice, and beans. These health-promoting foods should not be confused with highly processed carbohydrate sources such as white flour or table sugar. When you eat whole foods, you're consuming the phytonutrients and fiber that accompany the carbohydrates, so they don't have the same deleterious effects as processed carbs.

In fact, type 2 diabetes, which is often associated with a low-carb diet, has been shown to respond extremely well to a WFPB diet. A study in *Diabetes Care* found that "a diet rich in carbohydrate and fiber, essentially based on legumes, vegetables, fruits, and whole cereals, may be particularly useful for treating diabetic patients," because it increases their sensitivity to the insulin they're already producing.

FAT

Some diets recommend maximizing fats, while others look to minimize it. As in the case of protein and carbohydrates, fat is best consumed in its whole plant form. While generally lower in fat than the standard American diet (SAD), WFPB diets based around whole grains, legumes, fruits, and vegetables provide around 10 to 20 percent fat from calories. This percentage is consistent with recommendations found in many studies researching a WFPB diet's beneficial effects on lowering cholesterol, reversing heart disease, and treating type 2 diabetes. Higher-fat plant foods such as nuts, seeds, and avocados, while not necessarily required, are regularly included in smaller amounts on a WFPB diet. You will find many of these higher-fat plant foods listed as ingredients for plant-based milks, sauces, desserts, and entrées.

OTHER NUTRIENTS

Meeting the requirements for many vitamins, minerals, and nutrients on a WFPB diet is purely a matter of eating a variety of whole plant foods. Below, you'll find a list of some great whole foods that are known to contain adequate amounts of various nutrients. This list by no means contains all existing plant foods rich in nutrients, but it should give you an idea of the vast number of ways people following a WFPB diet can meet their nutrition needs. If you're concerned about meeting your needs for a specific vitamin, mineral, or nutrient, ask your health care provider to perform a blood test.

NUTRIENT	FOOD
VITAMIN A	Carrots, sweet potato, spinach, cantaloupes, bell peppers, mangos
VITAMIN C	Bell peppers, broccoli, citrus, strawberries, kiwis,

	Brussels sprouts
VITAMIN D	Mushrooms, fortified plant milks, sun exposure
VITAMIN E	Nuts, seeds, tomatoes, spinach, broccoli
CALCIUM	Greens (spinach, collard, kale, turnip), legumes
FOLATE	Rice, beans, greens, asparagus, Brussels sprouts, avocados, broccoli
IRON	Legumes, spinach, beet greens
ZINC	Soy, legumes, whole grains, pumpkin seeds, cashews

SUPPLEMENTS

Because a WFPB diet has such a high density of vitamins, minerals, and nutrients, there is only one supplement that is recommended by most doctors prescribing a plant-based diet. That supplement is vitamin B_{12}. Produced by microorganisms, B_{12} was historically consumed by unwittingly eating the residual soil on harvested plants and in natural water supplies. But in our current sanitized food and water systems, as much as 39 percent of the population, including both vegans and meat eaters, is in the low normal to deficient range for B_{12}. Many factors, including age, gender, and lifestyle, affect the recommended intake of vitamin B_{12}, but the current recommended daily dose for healthy adults is about 2.4 micrograms.

> For a healthy WFPB diet sufficient in nutrients, eat a wide variety of foods. This will also help keep your meals exciting as you take steps toward making this way of eating more of a lifestyle than a diet.

When You Don't Feel Like Cooking

Adopting a whole-food, plant-based diet doesn't necessarily mean cooking everything from scratch or never stepping foot in a restaurant again. You can still enjoy the pleasures of eating out and the convenience of packaged foods —you'll just have to put a little more thought into your orders and purchases. The tips that follow may not work exactly the same at every restaurant or grocery store, but they're a good starting point. As you begin looking into your local WFPB options, try to not only plan ahead but also be creative.

PACKAGED FOOD

On the one hand, packaged foods can be a big help when it comes to sticking with a WFPB diet. It's important to note that the following foods should not make up the bulk of a WFPB diet, but by choosing the right convenience foods to stock your pantry or refrigerator with, you can set yourself up for success. A few of the packaged foods that can be a great addition to a WFPB diet include oil-free whole-grain breads, whole-grain pastas, corn tortillas, no-salt-added canned beans, and frozen vegetables.

On the other hand, there are also packaged foods that can keep you from reaching your WFPB health goals. Avoid anything containing added salt, oil, or sugar—many packaged foods contain all three! Common foods to avoid include cookies, potato and tortilla chips, oil-filled salad dressings, and frozen dinners.

While looking at the nutrition facts on a food's label can be helpful, an even better approach is to look at the ingredients list. If there are animal products (e.g., milk, casein, whey, lard, anchovies, lactic acid, or gelatin), ingredients you don't recognize as being from whole foods, or dozens of ingredients, you want to look for a better option.

ORDERING AT A RESTAURANT

While purchasing WFPB packaged foods from the grocery store is a bit like a scavenger hunt, ordering food at a restaurant can be more like a dance. Many restaurants now have menus either partly or completely dedicated to vegan items, but many times these vegan items are just as full of salt, oil, and sugar as the regular menu items. So, whether you find yourself in a steakhouse for a work outing or at a local vegetarian restaurant, there are a few key tips and tricks to ordering while eating out.

If you know ahead of time that you'll be eating at a particular restaurant, you can check their online menu or call in. Through a simple phone call, you can normally find out if they have anything on the regular menu that will fit your needs or whether the chef would be willing to make a special WFPB entrée for you. This route may not work at every restaurant, but you might be surprised by the number of chefs who would love to create a healthy WFPB meal, given enough time to plan ahead.

If you don't have the convenience of planning ahead, the best place to look on a restaurant menu is the sides. Most restaurants will have various vegetables and starches that can be steamed or baked without oil and butter. A baked potato topped with steamed broccoli and a side salad (order the dressing on the side to ensure it's truly oil-free) not only makes a healthy meal, but also gives you a good chance of having the smallest bill at the table.

OTHER WAYS TO TAKE A BREAK FROM COOKING

- **Doubling or tripling recipes** when cooking dinner is a great way to stock up on ready-to-heat meals for the following days.
- **Keeping cooked starchy staples** (e.g., rice, beans, potato, and sweet potato) in the refrigerator means you're never more than a few minutes away from a warm and satisfying WFPB meal.
- **Batch-cooking and then freezing** is another great way to stock up on future lunches or dinners for when your schedule gets hectic.
- **Organizing potlucks** can be a great way to lessen the load and get family and friends involved in cooking WFPB meals.

HEALTHY NO-COOK SNACKS

Beyond keeping healthy staple foods and cooked meals in the refrigerator or freezer, having ideas for healthy no-cook snacks is a great way to stay on track with a WFPB diet. Families with children may find it especially helpful to have convenient snacks around the house. The best snacks are in their minimally processed, whole-food form. This could mean keeping fresh fruits like bananas and apples always stocked on the countertop. A homemade trail mix made of dried fruits, nuts, and granola (here) is also a great option for a snack that travels well. When snacking at work or home, try keeping a bag of sliced vegetables (e.g., carrots, peppers, and celery) ready to dip in some homemade White Bean and Chickpea Hummus (here).

Tips and Tricks

Here are a few tips and tricks to help keep you happy and healthy as you embark on your WFPB journey.

- **It's okay to keep it simple.** As your taste buds and palate develop, you may begin using more exotic recipes and ingredients, but when you're just getting started, feel free to stick to WFPB recipes and ingredients you're already familiar with.

- **Always be prepared.** Keep your pantry, refrigerator, and freezer full of ready-to-heat-and-eat staples like rice, beans, whole-grain pasta, rolled oats, frozen fruits, and frozen vegetables.

- **Get to know your local international grocery stores.** Many times, by stepping into an Asian, Middle Eastern, or European market, you can find varieties of whole grains, legumes, fruits, and vegetables that are unavailable in traditional grocery stores. The prices for bulk items are often very reasonable, and learning about new ingredients can keep a WFPB diet fresh and exciting.

- **Keep only WFPB ingredients at home and in the kitchen.** This is one of the best ways to ensure that you stay committed to this way of eating.

- **Try making WFPB versions of meals.** If you're the primary cook in the family, start with WFPB versions of meals they already love. Beginning your WFPB journey in a home with others who are not yet ready to make the switch can make things a bit more complicated, but it's certainly doable. If you receive a lot of pushback, you can always prepare the staples in a WFPB manner and then allow others to doctor them up in the way they'd prefer.

- **Allow yourself a certain level of grace.** Whether you're just beginning or have been eating a WFPB diet for many years, be kind with yourself. After a period of making what might not have been the best dietary choices, the key is to focus back in and ensure that your next meal aligns with your healthy WFPB lifestyle.

> *Gradually easing into a WFPB diet or making the switch all at once are both valid ways to get started. However, individuals whose medical care providers have prescribed a WFPB diet for various health concerns should consider making the necessary steps to adopt a WFPB diet as quickly as possible.*

You Can Do It!

As someone taking the first step toward adopting a WFPB diet, you're well on your way to enjoying its many benefits. We previously covered the various health conditions a WFPB diet has been shown to help prevent or treat, how it can help lower your monthly food budget, and its impact on animals and the environment. By eating a wide variety of whole plant foods, you'll soon find that a WFPB diet is much more about exploration than deprivation.

It's important to note that there are benefits for everyone looking into a WFPB diet, whether you're trying to add a few WFPB meals into your weekly menu, help a family member suffering from a chronic disease, or set your children or other loved ones on a path toward health and longevity. If you're interested in getting connected with other individuals or families who are also eating a WFPB diet, a wonderful place to look is the internet. There are vast numbers of groups on social media and other websites that exist to help others successfully continue their WFPB journey.

INSTEAD OF THIS, EAT THAT

NON-WFPB FOODS	WFPB ALTERNATIVES
DAIRY MILK	Plant-based milks (here or here)
SCRAMBLED EGGS	Scrambled tofu (here)
EGG WHITES	Aquafaba (cooked bean liquid)
PARMESAN CHEESE	Sunflower Parmesan "Cheese"
SOUR CREAM	Plant-Powered "Sour Cream"
CHEESE SAUCE/QUESO	Anytime "Cheese" Sauce
TABLE SUGAR	Date sugar
GELATIN	Agar-agar powder
HONEY	Maple syrup
ICE CREAM	Nice cream (here or here)
HAMBURGERS	Bean burgers (here) or Falafel Burgers
SHREDDED MEATS	Jackfruit (here)
SPAGHETTI SAUCE WITH BEEF	Easy One-Pot Vegan Marinara

The Plant-Based Kitchen

Next, I'll introduce some of the kitchen tools and common ingredients that you may want to have on hand as you begin your exciting new plant-based journey. Many of the tools and ingredients can be substituted with similar items that may be more available depending on your location.

SHOPPING TIPS

Take an inventory. It's helpful to run a quick inventory of your current stock in the kitchen and pantry. Doing so helps avoid food waste from items going stale or expiring and can help you keep track of which items you're running low on and need to resupply.

Make a list. Grocery shopping can be a highlight of the week for some and a chore for others. Either way, it pays to have a plan before making the trip. Research shows that you can save both time and money at the grocery store by having a plan in the form of a shopping list.

Don't shop on an empty stomach. After making a list and checking the current state of your pantry, try timing your shopping after a meal. Many people have experienced regret while unpacking groceries purchased on an empty stomach.

Buy in bulk. After you've been following a WFPB diet for a while, you'll more than likely have a few staple foods that you eat as the base of many of your meals, such as oats, potatoes, rice, or beans. Buying these foods in bulk saves you money and can also help save space in the shopping cart, as you may only need to purchase them once a month or so.

> *Just because WFPB recipes don't contain any added salt, oil, or sugar doesn't mean they have to be bland! Begin looking at herbs and spices as a way to add flavor and finesse to your meals.*

INGREDIENTS LIST VS. NUTRITION LABEL

While the best place to do the majority of your shopping will be the produce and dry goods section, you will of course find yourself in some of the center aisles of the grocery store. This is where learning to read the ingredients list and then the nutrition label is so important.

The ingredients list gives you a much clearer look at what's truly going into the product by listing all the ingredients in order from the largest quantity to the smallest. Once you've looked at the ingredients, you'll be able to see whether it supports your WFPB diet or should go back on the shelf.

The reason the nutrition label is less important is that food manufacturers skew the figures by using unrealistic serving sizes that can keep certain nutrients from meeting the minimum amount required to be listed. This is how companies are able to list products like nonstick cooking sprays as being "fat-free" and "zero calories," even though the main ingredient is oil!

PANTRY ESSENTIALS

The following items are just a few of the many different food options available to you on a WFPB diet. You may find that you use most of these foods or that you prefer other whole foods. The key is that you keep a wide variety of foods and spices in your pantry so that you are well prepared to make the recipes in this book.

dry goods

- Beans (black, great northern, kidney, navy, pinto, etc.)
- Brown rice (basmati, jasmine, long-grain, short-grain, etc.)
- Chickpeas
- Lentils (black, brown, green, red, yellow)
- Oats (old-fashioned, quick-cooking, steel-cut)
- Quinoa
- Split peas (green, yellow)
- Whole-grain pasta (angel hair, shells, spaghetti, etc.)

starchy vegetables

- Beets
- Carrots
- Corn
- Peas

- Radishes
- Squash (acorn, butternut, spaghetti, etc.)
- Sweet potatoes
- Turnips
- White potatoes

non-starchy vegetables

- Asparagus
- Bell pepper
- Broccoli
- Brussels sprouts
- Cabbage
- Cauliflower
- Celery
- Cucumber
- Eggplant
- Garlic
- Green beans
- Hot peppers
- Leafy greens (arugula, chard, collards, kale, lettuce, spinach, etc.)
- Mushrooms
- Onion
- Tomato

fruit

- Apples
- Bananas
- Berries (blackberry, blueberry, strawberry, etc.)

- Citrus (grapefruit, lemon, lime, orange, etc.)
- Dried fruit (prunes, raisins, etc.)
- Grapes
- Kiwi
- Melons (cantaloupe, honeydew, watermelon, etc.)

canned goods (look for no-salt-added & bpa-free)

- Beans
- Pumpkin purée
- Tomato paste
- Young green jackfruit

spices

- Black pepper, freshly ground
- Chili powder
- Cinnamon, ground
- Cumin, ground
- Curry powder (look for salt-free versions)
- Garlic powder
- Ginger, ground
- Nutritional yeast
- Onion powder
- Oregano, dried
- Paprika
- Sage, dried
- Salt-free seasoning
- Thyme, dried
- Turmeric, ground

liquids

- Balsamic vinegar
- Herbal teas (ginger, hibiscus, lemon, mint, etc.)
- Maple syrup
- Rice vinegar
- Vanilla extract

REFRIGERATOR AND FREEZER ESSENTIALS

refrigerator

Many items listed as pantry essentials, like leafy greens and mushrooms, should be stored in the refrigerator. Beyond fresh vegetables and fruits, other convenience items like condiments and precooked items can also be found in a WFPB refrigerator.

- Baked potatoes (here)
- BBQ Sauce (here)
- Cooked beans (here)
- Cooked brown rice (here)
- Corn tortillas
- Homemade salad dressings (here , here , and here)
- Hot sauce
- Ketchup (here)
- Leftovers
- Plant-based milks (almond, cashew [here], oat [here], rice, soy)

freezer

For busy individuals and families, having a fully stocked freezer can help make quick, easy, and delicious WFPB meals a reality. Frozen fruits can be added to oatmeals and smoothies or be made into desserts like nice creams.

Frozen vegetables can be steamed, microwaved, or roasted in just a few minutes before being added to a recipe or served as a side.

- Broccoli
- Brussels sprouts
- Carrots
- Cauliflower
- Corn
- Frozen fruit
- Green beans
- Hash browns or diced potatoes (make sure there's no added oil)
- Onions
- Peas
- Peppers
- Spinach
- Squash

HOW TO COOK THE BASICS

A healthy WFPB diet is built around simple starchy staples. These can be cooked in many ways using common kitchen tools and appliances. By finding your favorite ways to regularly prepare starchy staples, you can have healthy, ready-to-warm foods always available.

	METHOD	RATIO OF STAPLE TO WATER	SETTING AND COOK TIME	YIELD (FOR 1 CUP DRY STAPLE)
	Stovetop	1:2	Bring to boil, then simmer, covered, for 30 minutes	
Brown rice	Pressure cooker	1:1¼	Manual for 15 minutes	2 cups
	Slow	1:1½	High for 2½ hours	

	cooker		Low for 5 hours	
	Stovetop	1:1½	Bring to boil, then simmer, covered, for 20 minutes	
Quinoa	Pressure cooker	1:1	Manual for 1 minute	3 cups
	Slow cooker	1:1½	High for 2½ hours	
			Low for 5 hours	
	Oven	—	400°F for 40 to 50 minutes	
Potato, whole (e.g., red, white, yellow)	Stovetop	Water to cover all potatoes	Boil, covered, for 20 to 30 minutes	N/A
	Pressure cooker	1 cup water	Manual for 10 to 15 minutes	
	Slow cooker	1 to 2 tablespoons water	High for 2 to 3 hours Low for 4 to 6 hours	
	Oven	—	400°F for 40 to 50 minutes	
Sweet potato, whole	Stovetop	Water to cover all sweet potatoes	Boil for 20 to 30 minutes	N/A
	Pressure cooker	1 cup water	Manual for 15 to 20 minutes	
	Slow cooker	1 to 2 tablespoons water	High for 4 hours Low for 6 hours	

	Stovetop	1:3	Soak overnight, then bring to boil and simmer for 45 to 60 minutes	
Beans	Pressure cooker	1:3	Dry: Manual for 25 to 30 minutes Soaked: Manual for 8 to 10 minutes	2¼ cups
	Slow cooker	1:3	Soak overnight, then cook on high for 3 to 4 hours or low for 6 to 8 hours	
	Stovetop	1:3	Bring to boil, reduce heat, and simmer for 25 minutes	
Lentils	Pressure cooker	1:3	Dry: Manual for 10 minutes Soaked: N/A	2½ cups
	Slow cooker	1:3	High for 3 to 4 hours Low for 6 to 8 hours	
	Stovetop	1:3	Soak overnight, bring to boil, and simmer for 35 to 40 minutes	
Chickpeas	Pressure cooker	1:3	Dry: Manual for 35 to 40 minutes Soaked: Manual for 10 to 15 minutes	2½ to 3 cups
	Slow cooker	1:3	Soak overnight, then cook on high for 3 to 4 hours or low for 6 to 8 hours	

	Oven	—	Bake on parchment paper–lined baking sheet for 25 to 30 minutes at 400°F	
Squash, diced (e.g., acorn, butternut, kabocha)	Stovetop	Water to cover all squash	Boil, covered, for 10 to 15 minutes	N/A
	Pressure cooker	1 cup water	Manual for 5 minutes	
	Slow cooker	1 to 2 tablespoons water	High for 3 hours Low for 6 hours	

ESSENTIAL EQUIPMENT

These are the kitchen tools that will be referenced and used quite often in the recipe chapters to follow. Hopefully many of these tools are already in your kitchen, but if not, you can manage most of the recipes by using a different tool or technique. For example, a slow cooker, electric pressure cooker, and stockpot can all be used interchangeably; you'd just have to adjust the cooking time.

utensils and tools

- Cutting board
- Mixing bowl
- Mixing spoons
- Set of sharp knives
- Slotted spoon
- Spatula
- Tongs

cookware

- Baking dishes (round, square, rectangle, and muffin tins)
- Baking sheets (look for stainless steel)
- Saucepans and skillets
- Steaming basket
- Stockpots

appliances

- Blender
- Oven
- Stove

NICE-TO-HAVE EQUIPMENT

The essential equipment will work for almost all of the recipes to follow. That being said, there are some other kitchen accessories that you may want to look into purchasing. This set of equipment can make the cooking process easier or take most of the work out of prepping. When looking for "nice-to-have" equipment, try to look for versions that are able to perform multiple tasks. For instance, some electric pressure cookers also have the ability to slow cook, cook rice, and sauté.

- Air fryer
- Electric pressure cooker
- Food processor
- Grill
- Immersion blender
- Nonstick frying pan (look for Teflon-free versions such as ceramic pans)
- Slow cooker
- Stand mixer

About the Recipes

Congratulations once again for making the choice to begin a WFPB diet! As you finish up the first chapter, you're now one step closer to enjoying all the wonderful benefits a WFPB diet has to offer. Before we get there, though, I want to reiterate that the following recipes will be free from all animal products, salt, oil, and sugar. But remember, as you're beginning your journey, choosing to sprinkle some salt on top of your cooked foods can help bridge the gap while you move toward an SOS-free, WFPB way of eating.

The majority of ingredients used in the following recipes will be whole foods, but there will also be some lightly processed plant-based foods such as tofu and whole-grain pasta. These recipes are designed with the beginner in mind, but experienced cooks can appreciate them as well. With some basic kitchen knowledge, you'll be able to transform these simple ingredients into healthy and delicious WFPB meals. You will hopefully see firsthand that a WFPB diet is much more about exploration than deprivation!

In the next chapters, you'll notice a few labels that appear throughout the recipes. They are as follows:

- **5 Ingredients:** Recipes with this label use no more than five ingredients.
- **1 Pot:** These recipes use only a single cooking vessel (e.g., pot, pan, bowl).
- **30 Minutes or Less:** This label indicates a recipe that takes 30 minutes or less to prep and cook, from start to finish.
- **Gluten Free:** These recipes do not use any ingredients containing gluten (or offer a simple gluten-free substitute).
- **Nut Free:** These recipes either don't use nuts or have a nut-free substitution tip attached.

Southwest Sweet Potato Skillet

CHAPTER 2
Shopping List and Sample Menu

To help make your transition to a WFPB diet as easy and enjoyable as possible, this chapter contains a sample shopping list and weekly menu. If you're looking for a first step, following this sample menu is a great place to start. Remember, the better prepared you are and the more you plan ahead, the easier it is to make WFPB a lifestyle and not just a diet.

Shopping List

starchy staples

- Black beans, dried (2 pounds)
- Brown rice, uncooked (2 pounds)
- Carrots (9)
- Corn, frozen, 3 (10-ounce) bags
- Corn tortillas, 1 (1-pound) bag
- Green peas, frozen, 2 (10-ounce) bags
- Oats, quick-cooking (4 ounces)
- Oats, rolled (8 ounces)
- Popcorn kernels, 1 (4-ounce) package
- Potatoes, white (6)
- Potatoes, Yukon Gold (4)
- Quinoa, uncooked, 1 (16-ounce) bag
- Split peas, dried, 1 (16-ounce) bag
- Sweet potatoes (3)
- Whole-grain bread, sliced (1 loaf)
- Whole-grain bread, unsliced (1 loaf)
- Whole-wheat flour, 1 (5-pound) bag
- Whole-wheat hamburger buns, 1 package of 8
- Whole-wheat macaroni pasta (1 pound)
- Whole-wheat slider buns, 1 package of 8

non-starchy vegetables

- Bell peppers (6)
- Broccoli (1 head)
- Cabbage, purple (1 head)
- Garlic (2 heads)
- Green beans, fresh (1½ pounds)
- Jalapeño (1)
- Kale (2 large bunches)
- Lettuce (2 heads)
- Mushrooms (1 pound)
- Scallions (1 bunch)
- Spinach (2 bunches)
- Sweet onions (4)
- Tomatoes (2)

fruit

- Avocados (2)
- Bananas (10)
- Lemon (1 large)
- Lime (1)
- Mango (1)
- Oranges (2), or orange juice
- Peach (1)
- Pineapples (2)
- Strawberries (1 pint)

- Watermelon (1 small)

canned goods

- Tomato paste, 2 (6-ounce) cans
- Young green jackfruit, 2 (20-ounce) cans

spices and herbs

- Basil, dried
- Black pepper, freshly ground
- Chili powder
- Cilantro, fresh (1 bunch)
- Cinnamon, ground
- Cumin, ground
- Dill, dried
- Garlic powder
- Ginger, fresh, 1 (2-inch) piece
- Nutritional yeast flakes
- Onion powder
- Oregano, dried
- Peppermint extract
- Poppy seeds
- Red pepper flakes
- Smoked paprika
- Thyme, dried

liquids

- Apple cider vinegar
- Balsamic vinegar
- Maple syrup, 1 (8-ounce) bottle
- Plant-based milk, 2 (32-ounce) containers, or homemade (here or here)
- Salsa
- Vanilla extract
- Vegetable broth, low-sodium, 3 (32-ounce) containers

miscellaneous

- Baking powder (aluminum-free)
- Baking soda
- Chia seeds
- Cocoa powder
- Cornstarch
- Defatted peanut powder
- Molasses
- Nuts (cashews, walnuts)
- Tofu, firm or extra-firm, 3 (14-ounce) packages
- Tofu, silken, 1 (14-ounce) package

Sample Menu

	BREAKFAST	LUNCH	SNACK	DINNER
MONDAY	Paradise Island Overnight Oatmeal	Burrito Bowl with Oil-Free Tortilla Chips	Strawberry-Avocado Toast with Balsamic Glaze	Baked Mac and Peas Lemony Kale Salad
TUESDAY	A.M. Breakfast Scramble	Baked Mac and Peas (leftover)	Strawberry-Watermelon Ice Pops	Easy Vegan Pizza Bread Salad with Strawberry-Peach Vinaigrette
WEDNESDAY	Lean Green Chocolate Smoothie	2 roasted sweet potatoes (here) with steamed broccoli	Sliced vegetables with Plant-Powered Ranch	Easy Enchilada Bake Southwest Spinach Salad
THURSDAY	Walnut Crunch Banana Bread	Southwest Spinach Salad (leftover) with baked	Kale Chips	Savory Split Pea Soup Salad with Lemon and Poppy Seed Dressing

		potato (here)		
FRIDAY	Chocolate and Peanut Butter Quinoa	Hawaiian Luau Burgers	Bowl of fresh fruit	Orange-Glazed Tofu Salad with Roasted Garlic Dressing
SATURDAY	Plant-Powered Pancakes	Oil-Free Rice-and-Vegetable Stir-Fry	Chocolate-Peppermint Nice Cream	Southwest Stuffed Peppers Southwest Spinach Salad
SUNDAY	Loaded Breakfast Burrito	BBQ Jackfruit Sliders	Showtime Popcorn	Sunday Slow Roast Asian-Style Slaw with Maple-Ginger Dressing

Strawberry-Avocado Toast with Balsamic Glaze

the
PART TWO
recipes

Whole-Wheat Blueberry Muffins

CHAPTER 3
Breakfasts

Eating a WFPB breakfast is a wonderful way to start the day off right. And, contrary to popular belief, you can even add in some vegetables at breakfast time. You can also keep breakfast as simple as you'd like, whether or not you decide to reach for the broccoli. A couple of baked sweet potatoes with maple syrup and a sprinkle of cinnamon can be a great, simple option for starting the day. Make sure to have a glass of water while enjoying breakfast to ensure that you begin your day well hydrated.

Whole-Wheat Blueberry Muffins

Walnut Crunch Banana Bread

Plant-Powered Pancakes

Maple-Pecan Granola

Paradise Island Overnight Oatmeal

Pumpkin Pie Oatmeal

Chocolate and Peanut Butter Quinoa

A.M. Breakfast Scramble

Loaded Breakfast Burrito

Southwest Sweet Potato Skillet

Whole-Wheat Blueberry Muffins

MAKES 8 MUFFINS

30 MINUTES, NUT FREE • PREP TIME: 5 MINUTES • COOK TIME: 25 MINUTES

When it comes to breakfasts that travel well, muffins are always a great choice. These blueberry muffins not only make a delicious breakfast but also a fun addition to school lunches or a convenient snack to bring along on a hike.

½ cup plant-based milk (here or here)
½ cup unsweetened applesauce
½ cup maple syrup
1 teaspoon vanilla extract
2 cups whole-wheat flour
½ teaspoon baking soda
1 cup blueberries

1. Preheat the oven to 375°F.
2. In a large bowl, mix together the milk, applesauce, maple syrup, and vanilla.
3. Stir in the flour and baking soda until no dry flour is left and the batter is smooth.
4. Gently fold in the blueberries until they are evenly distributed throughout the batter.
5. In a muffin tin, fill 8 muffin cups three-quarters full of batter.
6. Bake for 25 minutes, or until you can stick a knife into the center of a muffin and it comes out clean. Allow to cool before serving.

PREPARATION TIP: Both frozen and fresh blueberries will work great in this recipe. The only difference will be that muffins using fresh blueberries will cook slightly quicker than those using frozen.

PER SERVING (1 MUFFIN)
Calories: 200; Total fat: 1g; Carbohydrates: 45g; Fiber: 2g; Protein: 4g

Walnut Crunch Banana Bread

MAKES 1 LOAF

PREP TIME: 5 MINUTES • COOK TIME: 1 HOUR, PLUS 30 MINUTES TO COOL

Whenever the topic of favorite baked breakfast foods comes up, banana bread always seems to be near the top of the list. This WFPB version of banana bread can be made easily using slightly freckled, ripe bananas to keep the loaf moist and baking soda to give a good rise. Walnut pieces also give a nice crunch and nutty flavor to the loaf that pairs incredibly well with the flavors of cinnamon and vanilla.

4 ripe bananas
¼ cup maple syrup
1 tablespoon apple cider vinegar
1 teaspoon vanilla extract
1½ cups whole-wheat flour
½ teaspoon ground cinnamon
½ teaspoon baking soda
¼ cup walnut pieces (optional)

1. Preheat the oven to 350°F.
2. In a large bowl, use a fork or mixing spoon to mash the bananas until they reach a puréed consistency (small bits of banana are fine). Stir in the maple syrup, apple cider vinegar, and vanilla.
3. Stir in the flour, cinnamon, and baking soda. Fold in the walnut pieces (if using).
4. Gently pour the batter into a loaf pan, filling it no more than three-quarters of the way full. Bake for 1 hour, or until you can stick a knife into the middle and it comes out clean.

5. Remove from the oven and allow to cool on the countertop for a minimum of 30 minutes before serving.

PER SERVING (⅛ LOAF)
Calories: 178; Total fat: 1g; Carbohydrates: 40g; Fiber: 5g; Protein: 4g

Plant-Powered Pancakes

MAKES 8 PANCAKES

30 MINUTES, NUT FREE • PREP TIME: 5 MINUTES • COOK TIME: 15 MINUTES

If pancakes are your weekend tradition, there's no need to change that just because you've adopted a WFPB diet. With the addition of cinnamon, maple syrup, and vanilla, these plant-powered pancakes are full of flavor while remaining light and fluffy.

1 cup whole-wheat flour
1 teaspoon baking powder
½ teaspoon ground cinnamon
1 cup plant-based milk (here or here)
½ cup unsweetened applesauce ¼ cup maple syrup
1 teaspoon vanilla extract

1. In a large bowl, combine the flour, baking powder, and cinnamon.
2. Stir in the milk, applesauce, maple syrup, and vanilla until no dry flour is left and the batter is smooth.
3. Heat a large, nonstick skillet or griddle over medium heat. For each pancake, pour ¼ cup of batter onto the hot skillet. Once bubbles form over the top of the pancake and the sides begin to brown, flip and cook for 1 to 2 minutes more.
4. Repeat until all of the batter is used, and serve.

VARIATION TIP: To add a fruity twist to this recipe, place a few blueberries on the batter right after pouring it onto the pan.

PER SERVING (2 PANCAKES)
Calories: 210; Total fat: 2g; Carbohydrates: 44g; Fiber: 5g; Protein: 5g

Maple-Pecan Granola

SERVES 4

5 INGREDIENTS, GLUTEN FREE • PREP TIME: 5 MINUTES • COOK TIME: 20 MINUTES, PLUS 30 MINUTES TO COOL

Most store-bought granolas are filled with oil and refined sugar, but luckily, you can make your own WFPB granola in just a few minutes. And once you get the hang of it, you can really make hundreds of different flavor variations using whole-food ingredients.

1½ cups rolled oats
¼ cup pecan pieces
¼ cup maple syrup
1 teaspoon vanilla extract
½ teaspoon ground cinnamon

1. Preheat the oven to 300°F. Line a baking sheet with parchment paper.
2. In a large bowl, combine the oats, pecan pieces, maple syrup, vanilla, and cinnamon. Stir until the oats and pecan pieces are completely coated.
3. Spread the mixture on the baking sheet in an even layer. Bake for 20 minutes, stirring once after 10 minutes.
4. Remove from the oven, and allow to cool on the countertop for 30 minutes before serving. The granola may still be a bit soft right after you remove it from the oven, but it will gradually firm up as it cools.

SERVING TIP: Once the granola has cooled, you can serve it with a splash of plant-based milk (here or here), add it to your oatmeal, or make a tasty trail mix by adding in some of your favorite dried fruits.

PER SERVING
Calories: 220; Total fat: 7g; Carbohydrates: 35g; Fiber: 4g; Protein: 5g

Paradise Island Overnight Oatmeal

SERVES 2

1 POT, GLUTEN FREE, NUT FREE • PREP TIME: 5 MINUTES, PLUS 4 HOURS OR OVERNIGHT TO SOAK

With just a few common fruits, this recipe will transport your breakfast to the tropics. Overnight oatmeal is a great option for those who have busy or early mornings that make preparing breakfast difficult. You can make it after work or before bed and know that a tasty breakfast will be waiting in the refrigerator come morning.

2 cups rolled oats
2 cups plant-based milk (here or here)
½ cup diced mango (fresh or frozen)
½ cup pineapple chunks (fresh or frozen)
1 banana, sliced
1 tablespoon maple syrup
1 tablespoon chia seeds

1. In a large bowl, mix together the oats, milk, mango, pineapple, banana, maple syrup, and chia seeds.
2. Cover and refrigerate overnight or for a minimum of 4 hours before serving.

MAKE-AHEAD TIP: Make this recipe early in the week—or even make a double recipe—and separate it into covered, single-serving containers so you'll have two to four days' worth of breakfasts ready to eat.

PER SERVING
Calories: 510; Total fat: 12g; Carbohydrates: 93g; Fiber: 15g; Protein: 14g

Pumpkin Pie Oatmeal

SERVES 4

1 POT, GLUTEN FREE, NUT FREE • PREP TIME: 5 MINUTES • COOK TIME: 35 MINUTES

One of the best ways to wish a house full of guests "season's greetings" is to wake them up to the smell of Pumpkin Pie Oatmeal. Steel-cut oats offer a great change of pace to rolled oats and are extremely versatile in the different ways they can be cooked.

3 cups plant-based milk (here or here)
1 cup steel-cut oats
1 cup unsweetened pumpkin purée
2 tablespoons maple syrup
1 teaspoon ground cinnamon
⅛ teaspoon ground cloves
⅛ teaspoon ground nutmeg

1. In a medium saucepan over medium-high heat, bring the milk to a boil. When a rolling boil is reached, reduce the heat to low, and stir in the oats, pumpkin purée, maple syrup, cinnamon, cloves, and nutmeg.
2. Cover and cook for 30 minutes, stirring every few minutes to ensure none of the oatmeal sticks to the bottom of the pot, and serve.

MAKE-AHEAD TIP: This recipe can be made ahead in a slow cooker or electric pressure cooker. Both allow you to add the ingredients the night before and set the cook time. In a slow cooker, use the low setting and cook for 6 to 8 hours. In a pressure cooker, use the manual setting and cook for 20 minutes.

PER SERVING
Calories: 218; Total fat: 5g; Carbohydrates: 38g; Fiber: 6g; Protein: 7g

Chocolate and Peanut Butter Quinoa

SERVES 2

1 POT, 5 INGREDIENTS, 30 MINUTES, GLUTEN FREE • PREP TIME: 5 MINUTES • COOK TIME: 10 MINUTES

Quinoa can make a great breakfast alternative to oats for those who are allergic to them or just looking to change things up a bit. This Chocolate and Peanut Butter Quinoa is great for kids who may be familiar with the flavor of popular breakfast cereals. And it can be made in just a few minutes, especially if you keep a supply of cooked quinoa in the refrigerator.

1 cup plant-based milk (here or here)
2 cups cooked quinoa (see here)
1 tablespoon maple syrup
1 tablespoon cocoa powder
1 tablespoon defatted peanut powder

1. In a medium saucepan over medium-high heat, bring the milk to a boil.
2. Once a rolling boil is reached, reduce the heat to low, and stir in the quinoa, maple syrup, cocoa powder, and peanut powder.
3. Cook, uncovered, for 5 minutes, stirring every other minute. Serve warm.

SERVING TIP: The recipe calls for 1 tablespoon maple syrup, but if you find that you would like it sweeter, you can always add in a bit more, or top it with a sliced banana.

PER SERVING
Calories: 339; Total fat: 8g; Carbohydrates: 53g; Fiber: 7g; Protein: 14g

A.M. Breakfast Scramble

SERVES 2

1 POT, 30 MINUTES, GLUTEN FREE, NUT FREE • PREP TIME: 5 MINUTES • COOK TIME: 15 MINUTES

There are few meals better at getting the whole family to jump out of bed on a Saturday morning than a tasty breakfast scramble. This scramble is great as a main breakfast dish or as a scrumptious side next to a fresh stack of pancakes.

1 (14-ounce) package firm or extra-firm tofu
4 ounces mushrooms, sliced
½ bell pepper, diced
2 tablespoons nutritional yeast
1 tablespoon vegetable broth or water
½ teaspoon garlic powder
½ teaspoon onion powder
⅛ teaspoon freshly ground black pepper
1 cup fresh spinach

1. Heat a large skillet over medium-low heat.
2. Drain the tofu, then place it in the skillet and mash it down with a fork or mixing spoon. Stir in the mushrooms, bell pepper, nutritional yeast, broth, garlic powder, onion powder, and pepper. Cover and cook for 10 minutes, stirring once after about 5 minutes.
3. Uncover, and stir in the spinach. Cook for an additional 5 minutes before serving.

VARIATION TIP: Feel free to add different spices for variety. Add ½ teaspoon each of cumin and chili powder to give a Mexican flair, or add a teaspoon or two of your favorite curry powder for an Indian-inspired scramble.

PER SERVING
Calories: 230; Total fat: 10g; Carbohydrates: 16g; Fiber: 7g; Protein: 27g

Loaded Breakfast Burrito

SERVES 2

1 POT, 30 MINUTES, GLUTEN FREE, NUT FREE • PREP TIME: 5 MINUTES • COOK TIME: 20 MINUTES

Vitamin D–rich mushrooms, fiber-filled vegetables, and protein-packed tofu scramble make this breakfast burrito a perfect way to start your day with plant-powered nutrition. Eat it right away, or make the filling ahead of time so you can fill up a tortilla for a tasty meal any time of day. Feel free to substitute or add in any other vegetables that you enjoy.

½ block (7 ounces) firm tofu
2 medium potatoes, cut into ¼-inch dice
1 cup cooked black beans (see here), drained and rinsed
4 ounces mushrooms, sliced
1 jalapeño, seeded and diced
2 tablespoons vegetable broth or water
1 tablespoon nutritional yeast
½ teaspoon garlic powder
½ teaspoon onion powder
¼ cup salsa
6 corn tortillas

1. Heat a large skillet over medium-low heat.
2. Drain the tofu, then place it in the pan and mash it down with a fork or mixing spoon.
3. Stir the potatoes, black beans, mushrooms, jalapeño, broth, nutritional yeast, garlic powder, and onion powder into the skillet. Reduce the heat to low, cover, and cook for 10 minutes, or until the potatoes can be easily pierced with a fork.

4. Uncover, and stir in the salsa. Cook for 5 minutes, stirring every other minute.
5. Warm the tortillas in a microwave for 15 to 30 seconds or in a warm oven until soft.
6. Remove the pan from the heat, place one-sixth of the filling in the center of each tortilla, and roll the tortillas into burritos before serving.

PER SERVING
Calories: 535; Total fat: 8g; Carbohydrates: 95g; Fiber: 21g; Protein: 29g

Southwest Sweet Potato Skillet

SERVES 4

1 POT, 30 MINUTES, GLUTEN FREE, NUT FREE • PREP TIME: 5 MINUTES • COOK TIME: 15 MINUTES

Breakfast skillets are a great way to start the day because of the many different ways they can be prepared. This one is packed full of flavor and still ready to eat in just 20 minutes. And if you have a house full of guests and a large enough pan, this recipe can be doubled or tripled to fill everyone's plates.

4 medium sweet potatoes, cut into ½-inch dice
8 ounces mushrooms, sliced
1 bell pepper, diced
1 sweet onion, diced
1 cup vegetable broth or water, plus 1 to 2 tablespoons more if needed
1 teaspoon garlic powder
½ teaspoon ground cumin
½ teaspoon chili powder
⅛ teaspoon freshly ground black pepper

1. Heat a large skillet over medium-low heat.
2. When the skillet is hot, put the sweet potatoes, mushrooms, bell pepper, onion, broth, garlic powder, cumin, chili powder, and pepper in it and stir. Cover and cook for 10 minutes, or until the sweet potatoes are easily pierced with a fork.
3. Uncover, and give the mixture a good stir. (If any of the contents are beginning to stick to the bottom of the pan, add 1 to 2 tablespoons of broth.)
4. Cook, uncovered, for an additional 5 minutes, stirring once after about 2½ minutes, and serve.

SERVING TIP: This skillet is great on its own, but it can be enhanced with some toppings. Some great choices are Roasted Jalapeño and Lime Guacamole , White Bean and Chickpea Hummus , hot sauce, or salsa.

PER SERVING
Calories: 158; Total fat: 1g; Carbohydrates: 34g; Fiber: 6g; Protein: 6g

15-Minute French Fries

CHAPTER 4
Soups, Salads, and Sides

A great way to ensure you have a variety of WFPB options is to have a stable of easy-to-make soup, salad, and side recipes. These can be eaten with other healthy plant foods or as a meal on their own if you're short on time. A great goal is to try as many of these recipes as possible as you begin your WFPB journey. But once you find a few recipes you like, feel free to focus on making them a mainstay in your menu.

- Lime-Mint Soup
- Savory Split Pea Soup
- Kale and Lentil Stew
- Four-Can Chili
- Vegan "Toona" Salad
- Lemony Kale Salad
- Southwest Spinach Salad
- Asian-Style Slaw with Maple-Ginger Dressing Whole-Wheat Pita Pockets
- Creamy Potato Salad
- Sautéed Collard Greens

Crispy Cauliflower Wings

Baked Taquitos with Fat-Free Refried Beans

15-Minute French Fries

Fluffy Mashed Potatoes with Gravy

Lime-Mint Soup

SERVES 4

1 POT, 5 INGREDIENTS, 30 MINUTES, GLUTEN FREE, NUT FREE • PREP TIME: 5 MINUTES • COOK TIME: 20 MINUTES

Broth-based soups can be just what the doctor ordered when the weather cools down or you are feeling a bit under the weather. This Lime-Mint Soup can be made in just a few minutes with five simple ingredients. While the soup is cooking, you can have a batch of brown jasmine rice cooking simultaneously on the stovetop or in a rice cooker.

4 cups vegetable broth
¼ cup fresh mint leaves, roughly chopped
¼ cup chopped scallions, white and green parts
3 garlic cloves, minced
3 tablespoons freshly squeezed lime juice

1. In a large stockpot, combine the broth, mint, scallions, garlic, and lime juice. Bring to a boil over medium-high heat.
2. Cover, reduce the heat to low, simmer for 15 minutes, and serve.

SERVING TIP: Lime-Mint Soup is great for sipping as a hot broth during the winter months, but it is best enjoyed over a bed of freshly cooked brown jasmine rice or quinoa.

PER SERVING
Calories: 55; Total fat: 2g; Carbohydrates: 5g; Fiber: 1g; Protein: 5g

Savory Split Pea Soup

SERVES 6

1 POT, GLUTEN FREE, NUT FREE • PREP TIME: 5 MINUTES, PLUS OVERNIGHT TO SOAK • COOK TIME: 50 MINUTES

This warm and savory soup has become a household favorite for cold winter days. It's delicious as is, but to make it your own, feel free to add in some more fresh vegetables like corn, carrots, or hot peppers to give it a kick. If this will be your first time shopping for split peas, they can normally be found in the same general area as the dried beans at your local grocery store.

1 (16-ounce) package dried green split peas, soaked overnight
5 cups vegetable broth or water
2 teaspoons garlic powder
2 teaspoons onion powder
1 teaspoon dried oregano
1 teaspoon dried thyme
¼ teaspoon freshly ground black pepper

1. In a large stockpot, combine the split peas, broth, garlic powder, onion powder, oregano, thyme, and pepper. Bring to a boil over medium-high heat.
2. Cover, reduce the heat to medium-low, and simmer for 45 minutes, stirring every 5 to 10 minutes. Serve warm.

VARIATION TIP: If you didn't have a chance to soak the split peas overnight, you can use them in their dried state. Simply add 1 extra cup of broth or water and cook for an additional 50 minutes.

PER SERVING
Calories: 297; Total fat: 2g; Carbohydrates: 48g; Fiber: 20g; Protein: 23g

Kale and Lentil Stew

SERVES 8

1 POT, GLUTEN FREE, NUT FREE • PREP TIME: 10 MINUTES • COOK TIME: 50 MINUTES

Lentils and kale are both plant powerhouses when it comes to fiber, flavor, and protein. Because they are both rich and hearty, this recipe is a fall favorite. The stew will thicken up as it cools, so if you're reheating leftovers, you may need to add in a bit more water or vegetable broth when you warm it up.

5 cups (2 pounds) brown or green dry lentils
8 cups vegetable broth or water
4 cups kale, stemmed and chopped into 2-inch pieces
2 large carrots, diced
1 tablespoon smoked paprika
2 teaspoons onion powder
2 teaspoons garlic powder
1 teaspoon red pepper flakes
1 teaspoon dried oregano
1 teaspoon dried thyme

1. In a large stockpot, combine the lentils, broth, kale, carrots, paprika, onion powder, garlic powder, red pepper flakes, oregano, and thyme. Bring to a boil over medium-high heat.
2. Cover, reduce the heat to medium-low, and simmer for 45 minutes, stirring every 5 to 10 minutes. Serve warm.

VARIATION TIP: This recipe can also be prepared using an electric pressure cooker. All you will need to do is combine the ingredients inside the pressure cooker, set it to manual, and cook for 30 minutes. Then allow the pressure to naturally release for 15 to 20 minutes. Make sure to give it a good stir before serving.

PER SERVING
Calories: 467; Total fat: 3g; Carbohydrates: 78g; Fiber: 31g; Protein: 32g

Four-Can Chili

SERVES 6

1 POT, GLUTEN FREE, NUT FREE • PREP TIME: 5 MINUTES • COOK TIME: 30 MINUTES

Chili recipes can be made as complex or as simple as you like. This particular chili was made to be as tasty as possible while using a minimal amount of ingredients. By using canned beans and tomatoes, you can throw this chili together in just a matter of minutes. Make this recipe your own by adding your favorite seasonings or diced hot peppers for a spicy kick.

1 (28-ounce) can crushed tomatoes
1 (15-ounce) can low-sodium black beans
1 (15-ounce) can low-sodium cannellini beans
1 (15-ounce) can low-sodium chickpeas
1 tablespoon chili powder
1 teaspoon garlic powder
1 teaspoon onion powder
½ teaspoon ground cumin
½ teaspoon red pepper flakes (optional)

1. In a large stockpot, combine the tomatoes, black beans, cannellini beans, and chickpeas and their liquids with the chili powder, garlic powder, onion powder, cumin, and red pepper flakes (if using). Bring the chili to a boil over medium-high heat.
2. Cover, reduce the heat to medium-low, simmer for 25 minutes, and serve.

VARIATION TIP: To use dried beans instead of canned, soak ½ cup each dried black beans, dried cannellini beans, and dried chickpeas overnight, then drain, rinse, and put them in the pot with 5 cups vegetable broth or water, the spices, and the tomatoes. After the chili comes to a boil, reduce the heat and simmer for 45 to 60 minutes, or until the beans are tender while still holding their form.

PER SERVING
Calories: 185; Total fat: 1g; Carbohydrates: 33g; Fiber: 13g; Protein: 11g

Vegan "Toona" Salad

SERVES 4

1 POT, 30 MINUTES, GLUTEN FREE, NUT FREE • PREP TIME: 10 MINUTES

Vegan "Toona" Salad is the perfect option for a filling salad that can be served over a bed of fresh greens or on top of steamed potatoes. It's also an easy lunchtime meal that can be cooked in advance and eaten throughout the week. The ripe avocado adds wonderful creaminess, and the mashed chickpeas provide a texture and look similar to traditional tuna salad.

3 cups cooked chickpeas (see here)
1 avocado, peeled and pitted
½ cup chopped red onion
¼ cup chopped celery
2 tablespoons Dijon mustard
1½ tablespoons freshly squeezed lemon juice
½ tablespoon maple syrup
1 teaspoon garlic powder

1. In a large bowl, combine the chickpeas and the avocado. Using a fork or a potato masher, smash them down until the majority of the chickpeas have been broken apart. (Note that you don't want to purée the chickpeas but simply smash them so they're able to absorb the rest of the flavors of the dish.)
2. Stir in the onion, celery, mustard, lemon juice, maple syrup, and garlic powder, making sure everything is thoroughly combined, and serve.

SERVING TIP: Vegan "Toona" Salad is great on top of freshly toasted whole-wheat bread as a traditional or open-faced sandwich. You may also enjoy adding a juicy slice of tomato, a lettuce leaf, a drizzle of balsamic glaze, or all three.

PER SERVING
Calories: 298; Total fat: 10g; Carbohydrates: 42g; Fiber: 13g; Protein: 13g

Lemony Kale Salad

SERVES 4

1 POT, 5 INGREDIENTS, 30 MINUTES, GLUTEN FREE, NUT FREE • PREP TIME: 10 MINUTES

It doesn't get much better than a crisp, citrus-filled salad during the warm summer months. Lemony Kale Salad goes great as a side next to a bowl of warm soup or a heartier meal like <u>**Homestyle Lentil Loaf with Maple-Balsamic Glaze**</u> . Once prepared, kale salads can be <u>stored</u> in the refrigerator for up to 4 days.

2 tablespoons freshly squeezed lemon juice
½ tablespoon maple syrup
1 teaspoon minced garlic
5 cups chopped kale

In a large bowl, whisk together the lemon juice, maple syrup, and garlic. Add the kale, massage it in the dressing for 1 to 2 minutes, and serve.

PREPARATION TIP: Make sure to thoroughly massage the kale with the dressing ingredients. This will give the kale a beautiful texture and get the lemon and garlic flavors properly incorporated.

PER SERVING
Calories: 51; Total fat: 0g; Carbohydrates: 11g; Fiber: 1g; Protein: 3g

Southwest Spinach Salad

SERVES 2

1 POT, 30 MINUTES, GLUTEN FREE, NUT FREE • PREP TIME: 10 MINUTES

This filling salad can be shared as a side or eaten as a main dish for lunch or dinner. Add your favorite grains, spices, and toppings to make it your own. If you're prepping this salad for a future meal, keep the salad portion and dressing portion separate until you're ready to eat.

½ **tablespoon balsamic vinegar**
½ **tablespoon BBQ Sauce (here)**
½ **teaspoon smoked paprika**
¼ **teaspoon red pepper flakes**
8 ounces fresh spinach
½ **cup black beans, cooked (see here)** ½ **cup brown rice, cooked (see here)** ½ **cup corn**
½ **tablespoon whole flaxseed or sesame seeds**

1. In a large bowl, whisk together the vinegar, BBQ sauce, paprika, and red pepper flakes.
2. Mix in the spinach, black beans, rice, and corn. Toss well to coat.
3. Top with the flaxseed right before serving.

PER SERVING
Calories: 197; Total fat: 4g; Carbohydrates: 34g; Fiber: 10g; Protein: 11g

Asian-Style Slaw with Maple-Ginger Dressing

SERVES 6

1 POT, 30 MINUTES, GLUTEN FREE, NUT FREE • PREP TIME: 10 MINUTES

Asian-style slaw is a fantastic option for a salad that you can make ahead of time to eat throughout the week or take along in a cooler for a camping trip. The salad base of cabbage, carrots, bell pepper, and cilantro are perfect vehicles for the ginger, garlic, and rice vinegar in the dressing. Make this salad your own by adding your favorite WFPB toppings such as sesame seeds or crushed peanuts.

2 tablespoons rice vinegar
1 tablespoon maple syrup
1 tablespoon freshly grated ginger
1 teaspoon freshly grated garlic
¼ teaspoon red pepper flakes (optional)
4 cups chopped purple cabbage
1 cup shredded carrots
1 red or yellow bell pepper, sliced
¼ cup chopped scallions, white and green parts
¼ cup roughly chopped fresh cilantro

1. In a large bowl, whisk together the vinegar, maple syrup, ginger, garlic, and red pepper flakes (if using).
2. Add the cabbage, carrots, bell pepper, scallions, and cilantro. Mix until the vegetables are well coated with dressing, and serve.

INGREDIENT TIP: Prepackaged coleslaw mixes containing shredded cabbage and carrots can be purchased at most grocery stores. This is a great option if you're short on time.

PER SERVING
Calories: 43; Total fat: 0g; Carbohydrates: 9g; Fiber: 2g; Protein: 1g

Whole-Wheat Pita Pockets

SERVES 4

5 INGREDIENTS, NUT FREE • PREP TIME: 30 MINUTES, PLUS 2 HOURS FOR THE DOUGH TO RISE • COOK TIME: 5 MINUTES

Pitas are a wonderful side for soups, stews, and curries. These can also be made and then used as a substitute for traditional bread in recipes like **Easy Vegan Pizza Bread**. Once proofed, pita dough can be stored in a freezer-safe container in the freezer for up to 3 months, enabling you to thaw and bake it whenever you're ready for warm, fresh pita pockets.

2 cups whole-wheat flour
1 (¼-ounce) packet fast-acting bread yeast
1 cup water

1. In a large bowl, combine the whole-wheat flour and yeast. Then slowly pour in the water while continually mixing until there is no dry flour left.
2. Remove the dough from the mixing bowl, and knead it on a clean surface for 8 to 10 minutes, or until slightly springy and soft.
3. Form the dough into a ball and transfer it to another large bowl. Cover the bowl with a kitchen towel. Allow to proof at room temperature for 2 hours, or until the dough has doubled in size.
4. Put the baking sheet or baking stone you'll be using in the oven, and preheat the oven to 450°F.
5. Evenly divide the dough ball into 4 pieces. Roll out each ball until the dough is roughly ¼ inch thick.

6. Using a hot pad, remove the baking sheet from the oven, and line it with parchment paper. Place the disks of dough on the baking sheet. Bake for 3 to 5 minutes, or until the pitas puff up and turn slightly golden brown.

TECHNIQUE TIP: You can make the kneading process much easier if you have a stand mixer or food processor with a dough attachment. Just add all the ingredients to the stand mixer bowl, attach the dough hook, and set the mixer on medium-low speed to knead the dough for 5 to 8 minutes.

PER SERVING
Calories: 266; Total fat: 2g; Carbohydrates: 53g; Fiber: 8g; Protein: 10g

Creamy Potato Salad

SERVES 4

GLUTEN FREE, NUT FREE • PREP TIME: 10 MINUTES • COOK TIME: 20 MINUTES, PLUS 50 MINUTES TO COOL AND CHILL

Potato salad is the perfect summertime side dish at a picnic or barbecue, and this recipe stores for up to 4 days in the refrigerator before you serve it. For a more traditional potato salad, add ½ cup chopped celery and ¼ cup chopped onions in step 4.

5 large red or golden potatoes, cut into 1-inch cubes
1 cup silken tofu or 1 large avocado
¼ cup chopped fresh chives
2 tablespoons Dijon mustard
½ tablespoon freshly squeezed lemon juice
½ teaspoon garlic powder
½ teaspoon onion powder
½ teaspoon dried dill
¼ teaspoon freshly ground black pepper

1. Bring a large pot of water to a boil over high heat. Immerse the potatoes in the hot water gently and carefully. Boil for 10 minutes, or until the potatoes can be easily pierced with a fork. Drain.
2. Put the potatoes in a large bowl, and refrigerate for a minimum of 20 minutes.
3. Meanwhile, put the tofu in a separate large bowl. Using a fork or mixing spoon, smash the tofu until creamy. Whisk in the chives, mustard, lemon juice, garlic powder, onion powder, dill, and pepper until well combined.

4. Stir the cooled potatoes into the creamy dressing. Mix gently until the potatoes are well coated. Refrigerate the dish for at least 30 minutes or until ready to serve.

PER SERVING
Calories: 341; Total fat: 1g; Carbohydrates: 74g; Fiber: 12g; Protein: 10g

Sautéed Collard Greens

SERVES 4

5 INGREDIENTS, GLUTEN FREE, NUT FREE • PREP TIME: 10 MINUTES • COOK TIME: 25 MINUTES

Collards are a great green that can be purchased year-round in the grocery store or at local markets during the spring and fall months. If they're not available, then kale, turnip greens, or cabbage will also work in this recipe. Sautéed greens often come out oily, but these collard greens leave out the oil and show how easy and delicious it can be to eat a WFPB, SOS-free diet.

1½ pounds collard greens
1 cup vegetable broth
½ teaspoon garlic powder
½ teaspoon onion powder
⅛ teaspoon freshly ground black pepper

1. Remove the hard middle stems from the greens, then roughly chop the leaves into 2-inch pieces.
2. In a large saucepan, mix together the vegetable broth, garlic powder, onion powder, and pepper. Bring to a boil over medium-high heat, then add the chopped greens. Reduce the heat to low, and cover.
3. Cook for 20 minutes, stirring well every 4 to 5 minutes, and serve. (If you notice that the liquid has completely evaporated and the greens are beginning to stick to the bottom of the pan, stir in a few extra tablespoons of vegetable broth or water.)

PER SERVING
Calories: 28; Total fat: 1g; Carbohydrates: 4g; Fiber: 2g; Protein: 3g

Crispy Cauliflower Wings

SERVES 6

GLUTEN FREE, NUT FREE • PREP TIME: 10 MINUTES • COOK TIME: 40 MINUTES

Cauliflower wings are the perfect side for game day or any other get-together that you may be hosting or attending. With gluten-free flour and nut-free milk, this recipe can be enjoyed by almost everyone. For best results, toss them in BBQ Sauce (here) immediately after removing them from the oven. You can also eat them as is or dip them in your favorite WFPB sauce, such as **Plant-Powered Ranch** .

1 cup oat milk (here)
¾ cup gluten-free or whole-wheat flour
2 teaspoons garlic powder
2 teaspoons onion powder
½ teaspoon paprika
¼ teaspoon freshly ground black pepper
1 head cauliflower, cut into bite-size florets

1. Preheat the oven to 425°F. Line a baking sheet with parchment paper.
2. In a large bowl, whisk together the milk, flour, garlic powder, onion powder, paprika, and pepper. Add the cauliflower florets, and mix until the florets are completely coated.
3. Place the coated florets on the baking sheet in an even layer, and bake for 40 minutes, or until golden brown and crispy, turning once halfway through the cooking process. Serve.

MAKE-AHEAD TIP: You can make large batches and freeze them to cook at a later date. To do so, in step 3, bake the coated cauliflower for only 20 minutes, then allow it to cool before putting it in a freezer-safe container. When ready to eat, place the cauliflower on a parchment paper–lined baking sheet, and cook for about 25 minutes.

PER SERVING
Calories: 96; Total fat: 1g; Carbohydrates: 20g; Fiber: 2g; Protein: 3g

Baked Taquitos with Fat-Free Refried Beans

SERVES 4

30 MINUTES, GLUTEN FREE, NUT FREE • PREP TIME: 5 MINUTES • COOK TIME: 25 MINUTES

You can make these taquitos in large batches ahead of time on game days or for holiday parties. They're perfect for dipping in your favorite salsa, **Roasted Jalapeño and Lime Guacamole**, or **Plant-Powered "Sour Cream"**.

2 cups pinto beans, cooked (see here)
1 teaspoon chili powder
1 teaspoon ground cumin
½ teaspoon garlic powder
½ teaspoon onion powder
¼ teaspoon red pepper flakes
12 corn tortillas

1. Preheat the oven to 400°F. Line a baking sheet with parchment paper.
2. Combine the beans, chili powder, cumin, garlic powder, onion powder, and red pepper flakes in a food processor or blender. Pulse or blend on low for 30 seconds, or until smooth, then set aside.
3. Place the tortillas on the baking sheet, and bake for 1 to 2 minutes. This helps soften the tortillas and makes rolling them much easier.
4. Remove the tortillas from the oven, then add a couple of heaping tablespoons of the refried beans to the bottom half of

each corn tortilla. Roll the tortillas tightly, and place them back on the baking sheet, seam-side down.
5. Bake for 20 minutes, turning once after about 10 minutes, and serve.

PER SERVING
Calories: 286; Total fat: 3g; Carbohydrates: 56g; Fiber: 13g; Protein: 12g

15-Minute French Fries

SERVES 6

5 INGREDIENTS, GLUTEN FREE, NUT FREE • PREP TIME: 10 MINUTES • COOK TIME: 1 HOUR, PLUS 30 MINUTES TO COOL

Although this recipe will initially take longer than 15 minutes, the goal is to batch-cook and refrigerate the potatoes so they're ready to be made into French fries in 15 minutes whenever you like. Early in the week, follow the recipe up to step 3, then store the baked potatoes in an airtight container in the refrigerator. When you're ready for fries, just follow steps 4 through 6, and you'll be enjoying WFPB French fries in just minutes.

2 pounds medium white potatoes
1 to 2 tablespoons no-salt seasoning

1. Preheat the oven to 400°F. Line a baking sheet with parchment paper.
2. Wash and scrub the potatoes, then place them on the baking sheet and bake for 45 minutes, or until easily pierced with a fork.
3. Remove the potatoes from the oven, and allow to cool in the refrigerator for about 30 minutes, or until you're ready to make a batch of fries.
4. Preheat the oven to 425°F. Line a baking sheet with parchment paper.
5. Slice the cooled potatoes into the shape of wedges or fries, then toss them in a large bowl with the no-salt seasoning.
6. Spread the coated fries out in an even layer on the baking sheet. Bake for about 7 minutes, then remove from the oven,

flip the fries over, and redistribute them in an even layer. Bake for another 8 minutes, or until the fries are crisp and golden brown, and serve.

TECHNIQUE TIP: The potatoes can be initially cooked in a number of ways other than baking them in the oven. They can be boiled for 12 minutes or steamed in an electric pressure cooker on manual for 10 minutes.

PER SERVING
Calories: 104; Total fat: 0g; Carbohydrates: 24g; Fiber: 4g; Protein: 3g

Fluffy Mashed Potatoes with Gravy

SERVES 6

30 MINUTES, GLUTEN FREE, NUT FREE • PREP TIME: 10 MINUTES • COOK TIME: 15 MINUTES

Adopting a WFPB diet doesn't mean giving up your favorite foods, but rather adapting the way you cook. Mashed potatoes and gravy are a fantastic side for any occasion and can also be eaten as a main course accompanied by a salad or steamed vegetables. This recipe can be doubled or even tripled to feed however many guests you're expecting.

FOR THE MASHED POTATOES

8 red or Yukon Gold potatoes, cut into 1-inch cubes
½ cup plant-based milk (here or here)
1 teaspoon garlic powder
1 teaspoon onion powder

FOR THE GRAVY

2 cups vegetable broth, divided
¼ cup gluten-free or whole-wheat flour ½ teaspoon garlic powder
½ teaspoon onion powder
¼ teaspoon freshly ground black pepper
¼ teaspoon dried thyme
¼ teaspoon dried sage

TO MAKE THE MASHED POTATOES

1. Bring a large stockpot of water to a boil over high heat, then gently and carefully immerse the potatoes. Cover, reduce the heat to medium, and boil for 15 minutes, or until the potatoes are easily pierced with a fork.
2. Drain the liquid, and return the potatoes to the pot. Using a potato masher or large mixing spoon, mash the potatoes until

smooth.

3. Stir in the milk, garlic powder, and onion powder.

TO MAKE THE GRAVY

1. Meanwhile, in a medium saucepan, whisk together ½ cup of broth and the flour. Once no dry flour is left, whisk in the remaining 1½ cups of broth.
2. Stir in the garlic powder, onion powder, pepper, thyme, and sage. Bring the gravy to a boil over medium-high heat, then reduce the heat to low.
3. Simmer for 10 minutes, stirring every other minute, and serve with the mashed potatoes.

SERVING TIP: Mashed potatoes and gravy make a wonderful side paired with Baked Mac and Peas or the Homestyle Lentil Loaf with Maple-Balsamic Glaze .

PER SERVING
Calories: 260; Total fat: 1g; Carbohydrates: 56g; Fiber: 4g; Protein: 8g

Southwest Stuffed Peppers

CHAPTER 5
Entrées

Many of these entrée recipes are based around a few simple starchy staples, including rice, beans, potatoes, and oats. These recipes will show you how you can easily transform a few simple ingredients into a wide variety of tasty WFPB meals. And while I recommend trying out many or all of these recipes, you'll soon find the recipes you like the best and make them part of your regular repertoire. Having a few "go-to" recipes can help you feel confident knowing you're never more than a few minutes away from a delicious and healthy WFPB meal.

- BBQ Jackfruit Sliders
- Hawaiian Luau Burgers
- Falafel Burgers
- Easy Vegan Pizza Bread
- Baked Mac and Peas
- Savory Sweet Potato Casserole
- BBQ Tofu and Mashed Potato Bowl
- Sunday Slow Roast
- Oil-Free Rice-and-Vegetable Stir-Fry

- Vegetable Spring Rolls with Spicy Peanut Dipping Sauce
- Orange-Glazed Tofu Bowl
- Mango-Ginger Chickpea Curry
- Italian Bean Balls
- Crispy Rice-and-Bean Tostadas
- Southwest Stuffed Peppers
- Easy Enchilada Bake
- Burrito Bowl with Oil-Free Tortilla Chips
- Homestyle Lentil Loaf with Maple-Balsamic Glaze

BBQ Jackfruit Sliders

SERVES 6

30 MINUTES, NUT FREE • PREP TIME: 10 MINUTES • COOK TIME: 15 MINUTES

Jackfruit is a great WFPB substitute for pulled or shredded meats. You'll need unripe young green jackfruit for this dish, due to its texture and ability to take on flavors. This recipe also works as a great topping for WFPB nachos, pizza, or burgers.

2 (20-ounce) cans young green jackfruit, drained and rinsed
½ cup BBQ Sauce (here)
1 teaspoon garlic powder
1 teaspoon onion powder
6 whole-wheat slider buns
Asian-Style Slaw with Maple-Ginger Dressing **, for topping**
Tomatoes, onions, and pickles, for topping (optional)

1. In a large bowl, use a fork or potato masher to smash the jackfruit until it has a shredded consistency.
2. Heat a medium stockpot over medium-low heat. Put the shredded jackfruit, BBQ sauce, garlic powder, and onion powder in the pot, and stir. Cook for 10 minutes, covered, stirring once after about 5 minutes. If the jackfruit begins sticking to the bottom of the pot, add in a few tablespoons of vegetable broth or water.
3. Uncover and cook for 5 minutes, stirring every few minutes.
4. Serve on whole-wheat slider buns with your favorite toppings.

COOKING TIP: BBQ Jackfruit can also be made in a slow cooker. Using all of the same ingredients, cook for 3 to 4 hours on high or 6 to 8 hours on low.

PER SERVING
Calories: 188; Total fat: 2g; Carbohydrates: 36g; Fiber: 11g; Protein: 7g

Hawaiian Luau Burgers

SERVES 8

30 MINUTES, NUT FREE • PREP TIME: 15 MINUTES • COOK TIME: 10 MINUTES

Here's a healthy WFPB version of the standard American diet SAD burger. Instead of grilling, you can also bake the patties on a parchment paper–lined baking sheet at 425°F for 25 to 30 minutes, flipping once halfway through.

3 cups cooked black beans (see here)
2 cups cooked brown rice (see here)
1 cup quick-cooking oats
¼ cup BBQ Sauce, plus more for serving (here)
¼ cup pineapple juice
1 teaspoon garlic powder
1 teaspoon onion powder
1 pineapple, cut into ¼-inch-thick rings
8 whole-wheat buns
Lettuce, tomato, pickles, and onion, for topping (optional)

1. Preheat the grill to medium-high heat.
2. In a large bowl, use a fork or mixing spoon to mash the black beans.
3. Mix in the rice, oats, BBQ sauce, the pineapple juice, garlic powder, and onion powder. Continue mixing until the mixture begins to hold its shape and can be formed into patties.
4. Scoop out ½ cup of bean mixture, and form it into a patty. Repeat until all of the bean mixture is used.
5. Place the patties on the hot grill, and cook for 4 to 5 minutes on each side, flipping once the burgers easily release from the

grill surface.

6. After you flip the burgers, place the pineapple rings on the grill, and cook for 1 to 2 minutes on each side.

7. Remove the burgers and pineapple rings from the grill. Place one patty and one pineapple ring on each bun along with a spoonful of the BBQ sauce and your favorite burger fixings, and serve.

PER SERVING
Calories: 371; Total fat: 3g; Carbohydrates: 71g; Fiber: 10g; Protein: 15g

Falafel Burgers

SERVES 8

NUT FREE • PREP TIME: 15 MINUTES • COOK TIME: 30 MINUTES

This WFPB version brings together all the familiar flavors of traditional falafel, but in a healthier way. For a healthy heat-and-eat option, follow the recipe through step 3, then cover the patties and freeze for up to 4 months.

3 cups cooked chickpeas (see here)
2 cups cooked brown rice (see here)
¼ cup vegetable broth
¼ cup chopped fresh parsley
1 tablespoon freshly squeezed lemon juice
2 teaspoons garlic powder
2 teaspoons onion powder
1½ teaspoons ground cumin
1 teaspoon ground coriander
¼ teaspoon freshly ground black pepper Whole-Wheat Pita Pockets or whole-wheat buns Lettuce, tomato, and onion, for topping (optional)

1. Preheat the oven to 425°F. Line a baking sheet with parchment paper.
2. In a food processor or blender, combine the chickpeas, rice, broth, parsley, lemon juice, garlic powder, onion powder, cumin, coriander, and pepper. Process on low for 30 to 45 seconds, or until the mixture can easily be formed into patties but isn't so well mixed that you create hummus. You may need to stop the processor and scrape down the sides once or twice.

3. Scoop out ½ cup of the chickpea mixture, and form it into a patty. Place the patty on the baking sheet. Repeat until all of the chickpea mixture is used.
4. Bake for 15 minutes. Flip the patties, cook for 12 to 15 minutes more, and serve on pita pockets or buns with your preferred toppings.

MAKE-AHEAD TIP: You can follow the recipe through step 3, then cover the patties and freeze them in a freezer-safe container for up to 4 months. This provides you with a healthy heat-and-eat option for those evenings when you're short on time and energy.

PER SERVING
Calories: 230; Total fat: 3g; Carbohydrates: 44g; Fiber: 8g; Protein: 10g

Easy Vegan Pizza Bread

SERVES 4

1 POT, 5 INGREDIENTS, 30 MINUTES, NUT FREE • PREP TIME: 5 MINUTES • COOK TIME: 20 MINUTES

The key to great pizza bread is finding a hearty vegan whole-wheat loaf to hold all your tasty toppings. This recipe is on the simple side, but you can always add more fresh ingredients before cooking, like sliced mushrooms, peppers, onions, pineapple, basil, or spinach. Once your pizza is cooked, try topping it with some **Sunflower Parmesan "Cheese"** or red pepper flakes for some extra heat.

1 whole-wheat loaf, unsliced
1 cup Easy One-Pot Vegan Marinara
1 teaspoon nutritional yeast
½ teaspoon onion powder
½ teaspoon garlic powder

1. Preheat the oven to 375°F.
2. Halve the loaf of bread lengthwise. Evenly spread the marinara onto each slice of bread, then sprinkle on the nutritional yeast, onion powder, and garlic powder.
3. Place the bread on a baking sheet and bake for 20 minutes, or until the bread is a light golden brown.

INGREDIENT TIP: If you're having a tough time finding a good whole-wheat loaf, or if you'd just prefer a thinner crust, you can easily substitute a tortilla shell or pita (here) for the loaf of bread.

PER SERVING
Calories: 230; Total fat: 3g; Carbohydrates: 38g; Fiber: 7g; Protein: 13g

Baked Mac and Peas

SERVES 8

5 INGREDIENTS, NUT FREE • PREP TIME: 15 MINUTES • COOK TIME: 40 MINUTES

Macaroni and cheese is a standard American diet (SAD) favorite that can be found on almost every child's plate. This Baked Mac and Peas is a healthy WFPB alternative that's sure to become a dinnertime favorite for kids and adults alike. Made with **Anytime "Cheese" Sauce**, this recipe can be doubled or tripled to suit any size guest list.

1 (16-ounce) package whole-wheat macaroni pasta
1 recipe Anytime "Cheese" Sauce
2 cups green peas (fresh or frozen)

1. Preheat the oven to 400°F.
2. In a large stockpot, cook the pasta per the package instructions for al dente. Drain the pasta.
3. In a large baking dish, combine the pasta, sauce, and peas, and mix well.
4. Bake for 30 minutes, or until the top of the dish turns golden brown.

COOKING TIP: If you'd prefer not to bake this recipe, it can always be prepared like a traditional macaroni and cheese. All you need to do is boil your noodles according to the package directions and then drain the water before stirring in the cheese sauce.

PER SERVING
Calories: 209; Total fat: 3g; Carbohydrates: 42g; Fiber: 7g; Protein: 12g

Savory Sweet Potato Casserole

SERVES 6

1 POT, 5 INGREDIENTS, GLUTEN FREE, NUT FREE • PREP TIME: 15 MINUTES • COOK TIME: 30 MINUTES

Sweet potatoes are an extremely versatile starchy staple. This casserole combines their natural sweetness with the savory flavors of sage, thyme, and rosemary. It goes great with almost any steamed vegetable but is particularly special served with a side of **Sautéed Collard Greens** .

8 sweet potatoes, cooked (see here)
½ cup vegetable broth
1 tablespoon dried sage
1 teaspoon dried thyme
1 teaspoon dried rosemary

1. Preheat the oven to 375°F.
2. Remove and discard the skin from the cooked sweet potatoes, and put them in a baking dish. Mash the sweet potatoes with a fork or potato masher, then stir in the broth, sage, thyme, and rosemary.
3. Bake for 30 minutes and serve.

PER SERVING
Calories: 154; Total fat: 0g; Carbohydrates: 35g; Fiber: 6g; Protein: 3g

BBQ Tofu and Mashed Potato Bowl

SERVES 4

5 INGREDIENTS, GLUTEN FREE, NUT FREE • PREP TIME: 15 MINUTES, PLUS 45 MINUTES TO SIT • COOK TIME: 10 MINUTES

Tofu can be used in many different ways, including as a saucy entrée perfect for pairing with starches and vegetables. This bowl is a great option for prepping at home and then bringing to a cookout, where you can grill the tofu. Marinate the tofu in any of your favorite WFPB sauces or dressings for dozens of different flavor possibilities for this dish.

1 (14-ounce) package firm or extra-firm tofu ¼ cup BBQ Sauce (here)
6 cups Fluffy Mashed Potatoes
1 recipe Gravy (here)

1. Remove the tofu from the water it's packaged in, and place it on a paper towel–lined plate. Then place a plate on top of the tofu and a bowl or mug on top of the plate to help weigh it down. Allow the tofu to be pressed for a minimum of 30 minutes and up to 2 hours.
2. Slice the tofu block into ½-inch slices.
3. In a large bowl, gently mix the tofu slices with the BBQ sauce until the tofu is coated. Allow the tofu to marinate for 15 minutes to 1 hour.
4. Preheat the grill or a grill pan on the stove to high heat. Grill the tofu slices for 4 to 5 minutes, then gently flip them over and grill for 4 to 5 minutes more, or until the tofu easily releases from the grill surface.

5. To serve, fill each of 4 bowls with 1½ cups of mashed potatoes, top with one-quarter of the grilled tofu, and smother in gravy.

SERVING TIP: Grilled barbecue tofu is a great accompaniment to many other WFPB dishes. Instead of serving it with mashed potatoes, you can add a slice to a Hawaiian Luau Burger , mix it into the Southwest Spinach Salad , or tuck a slice or two into a Loaded Breakfast Burrito .

PER SERVING
Calories: 336; Total fat: 5g; Carbohydrates: 61g; Fiber: 4g; Protein: 15g

Sunday Slow Roast

SERVES 8

GLUTEN FREE, NUT FREE • PREP TIME: 10 MINUTES • COOK TIME: 4 TO 6 HOURS

This recipe is the perfect slow-cooked meal to enjoy at the end of a busy weekend. For this tasty lunch or dinner recipe, all you need to do is put all the ingredients in the slow cooker and allow the magic to happen throughout the early morning and afternoon. Get creative and make it your own by adding in fresh vegetables from your garden or seasonal produce from the market.

6 medium white potatoes, cut into 1-inch cubes
6 large carrots, cut into ½-inch rounds
3 sweet onions, cut into ½-inch cubes
12 ounces green beans (fresh or frozen)
8 ounces mushrooms, sliced
4 cups vegetable broth
1 teaspoon onion powder
1 teaspoon garlic powder
1 teaspoon freshly ground black pepper

1. Put the potatoes, carrots, onions, green beans, mushrooms, broth, onion powder, garlic powder, and pepper in a slow cooker. Stir together so the spices are well distributed.
2. Cook for 4 hours on high or 6 to 8 hours on low.
3. Remove the lid and stir before serving.

TECHNIQUE TIP: To cook this recipe on the stovetop in a large stockpot or Dutch oven, in step 2, simply place the pot on the stovetop, and cook, covered, over low heat for 4 hours.

PER SERVING
Calories: 190; Total fat: 1g; Carbohydrates: 39g; Fiber: 8g; Protein: 8g

Oil-Free Rice-and-Vegetable Stir-Fry

SERVES 4

1 POT, 30 MINUTES, GLUTEN FREE, NUT FREE • PREP TIME: 5 MINUTES • COOK TIME: 15 MINUTES

One of the main ingredients in a traditional stir-fry is oil, but this recipe will show you how simple it can be to cook a stir-fry without it. Some other great vegetables to use in this recipe include broccoli florets, chopped or sliced carrots, onions, and mushrooms.

2 cups green peas (fresh or frozen)
2 cups green beans (fresh or frozen)
¼ cup vegetable broth or water
1 teaspoon garlic powder
1 teaspoon onion powder
4 cups brown rice, cooked (see here)

1. Heat a medium saucepan over medium heat.
2. Put the peas, green beans, broth, garlic powder, and onion powder in the pan, and stir. Cover and cook for 8 minutes, stirring every few minutes, or until crisp-tender. (If any of the vegetables begin sticking, stir in a few more tablespoons of vegetable broth or water.)
3. Uncover, and stir in the cooked brown rice. Cook for an additional 5 minutes, stirring every other minute, and serve. (Add a tablespoon or two of water or broth if anything begins sticking to the bottom of the pan.)

SUBSTITUTION TIP: Frozen vegetables are a great choice when making an oil-free stir-fry. You can sometimes find a "stir-fry mix" that includes a variety of vegetables, or you can swap out the green beans or peas for frozen broccoli, carrots, bell peppers, or cauliflower.

PER SERVING
Calories: 233; Total fat: 2g; Carbohydrates: 48g; Fiber: 7g; Protein: 8g

Vegetable Spring Rolls with Spicy Peanut Dipping Sauce

SERVES 2

30 MINUTES, GLUTEN FREE • PREP TIME: 15 MINUTES • COOK TIME: 10 MINUTES

Spring rolls are a great entrée that can be filled with a wide variety of fresh vegetables, cooked starches, and many different spices and herbs. They can be made on demand or prepared ahead of time for a potluck or picnic. In addition to the spring rolls, a spicy peanut dipping sauce adds an extra hit of flavor.

FOR THE SPICY PEANUT DIPPING SAUCE

2 tablespoons defatted peanut powder
1 tablespoon maple syrup
1 tablespoon rice vinegar
½ teaspoon onion powder
½ teaspoon garlic powder
½ teaspoon red pepper flakes

FOR THE SPRING ROLLS

6 (8- to 10-inch) rice paper wraps
6 large lettuce leaves
1½ cups brown rice, cooked (see here)
1 cup shredded carrots
1 bunch fresh cilantro
1 bunch fresh mint
1 bunch fresh basil

TO MAKE THE SPICY PEANUT DIPPING SAUCE

In a small saucepan over medium heat, combine the peanut powder, maple syrup, rice vinegar, onion powder, garlic powder, and red pepper flakes. Cook for 10 minutes, stirring occasionally. Remove the sauce from the heat, and set aside to cool.

TO MAKE THE SPRING ROLLS

1. Fill a shallow bowl or pan with warm water, and dip a rice paper wrap in the water for 10 to 15 seconds. Remove and place on a cutting board or other clean, smooth surface. (Note: The rice paper may not be completely soft right away, but it will soften as you add the filling.)
2. Lay a lettuce leaf down flat on a rice paper wrap, then add ¼ cup of brown rice, 2 to 3 tablespoons of shredded carrots, and a few leaves each of cilantro, mint, and basil.
3. Wrap the sides of the rice paper halfway into the center, then roll the wrap from the bottom to the top to form a tight roll.
4. Repeat for the remaining spring rolls. Serve with the sauce in a dipping bowl on the side.

VARIATION TIP: Chop up your favorite colorful vegetables to make this recipe your own. Some great options include purple cabbage, red and yellow bell peppers, scallions, avocado, and microgreens.

PER SERVING
Calories: 263; Total fat: 3g; Carbohydrates: 46g; Fiber: 5g; Protein: 11g

Orange-Glazed Tofu Bowl

SERVES 4

GLUTEN FREE, NUT FREE • PREP TIME: 15 MINUTES • COOK TIME: 40 MINUTES

This is a fantastic, healthy WFPB option for those nights when you're craving takeout. Other fruits or fruit juices can be substituted to give this recipe a fun twist, and if you have oranges on hand, you can squeeze the orange juice yourself. The tofu is served over a bed of cooked brown rice in this recipe, but it will also go great with the Oil-Free Rice-and-Vegetable Stir-Fry or cooked quinoa (see here).

FOR THE TOFU

¼ cup gluten-free or whole-wheat flour
1 teaspoon garlic powder
1 teaspoon onion powder
½ teaspoon freshly ground black pepper
1 (14-ounce) package firm or extra-firm tofu, drained and cut into ¼-inch cubes

FOR THE ORANGE GLAZE

½ cup orange juice, without pulp
1 tablespoon cornstarch
1 tablespoon rice vinegar
1 tablespoon maple syrup
½ teaspoon garlic powder
½ teaspoon onion powder

FOR THE BOWL

6 cups cooked brown rice (see here)

TO MAKE THE TOFU

1. Preheat the oven to 400°F. Line a baking sheet with parchment paper.

2. In a large bowl, whisk together the flour, garlic powder, onion powder, and pepper.
3. Toss the tofu with the flour and spices until completely coated.
4. Place the coated tofu on the baking sheet and bake for 40 minutes, turning after 20 minutes.

TO MAKE THE ORANGE GLAZE

While the tofu is baking, in a small saucepan, combine the orange juice, cornstarch, rice vinegar, maple syrup, garlic powder, and onion powder. Bring to a boil over medium-high heat. Reduce the heat to low, and simmer for 10 minutes. Remove from the heat and set aside to cool.

TO MAKE THE BOWL

1. Remove the tofu from the oven and gently mix it with the orange glaze.
2. To serve, put 1½ cups of cooked brown rice in each bowl, then top with one-quarter of the orange-glazed tofu.

VARIATION TIP: Follow the instructions to make the oil-free crispy tofu, then toss it in any other WFPB sauce or glaze. The unglazed tofu can also be served in a number of ways, including dipping it into some Sweet and Tangy Ketchup or BBQ Sauce, or adding it to a dinner bowl filled with mixed greens and starches.

PER SERVING
Calories: 380; Total fat: 8g; Carbohydrates: 65g; Fiber: 3g; Protein: 15g

Mango-Ginger Chickpea Curry

SERVES 6

1 POT, 30 MINUTES, GLUTEN FREE, NUT FREE • PREP TIME: 5 MINUTES • COOK TIME: 15 MINUTES

Curry is a comforting meal when the weather cools down in the fall or on a rainy spring day. Anyone can enjoy this one, regardless of their spice preferences, but if you like things more on the spicy side, feel free to add one or more chopped jalapeños or a teaspoon of red pepper flakes.

3 cups cooked chickpeas (see here)
2 cups mango chunks (fresh or frozen)
2 cups plant-based milk (here or here)
2 tablespoons maple syrup
1 tablespoon curry powder
1 tablespoon ground ginger
1 teaspoon ground coriander
1 teaspoon garlic powder
1 teaspoon onion powder
⅛ teaspoon ground cinnamon

1. Heat a large stockpot or Dutch oven over medium heat.
2. In the pot, combine the chickpeas, mango, milk, maple syrup, curry powder, ginger, coriander, garlic powder, onion powder, and cinnamon. Cover and cook for 10 minutes, stirring after about 5 minutes.
3. Uncover and cook for an additional 5 minutes, stirring every other minute. Serve.

TECHNIQUE TIP: You can cook this curry in an electric pressure cooker on manual for 30 minutes. It can also be prepared in a slow cooker on high for 4 to 6 hours. You could also just reduce the heat to low on the stovetop, and let it simmer for an extra 10 or 20 minutes.

PER SERVING
Calories: 219; Total fat: 4g; Carbohydrates: 38g; Fiber: 9g; Protein: 8g

Italian Bean Balls

SERVES 6

GLUTEN FREE, NUT FREE • PREP TIME: 10 MINUTES • COOK TIME: 30 MINUTES

Classic spaghetti and meatballs has long been a dinnertime staple. Serving these Italian Bean Balls with whole-wheat pasta and freshly made **Easy One-Pot Vegan Marinara** transforms this classic into a hearty, healthy WFPB dish. Don't forget to top your spaghetti and bean balls with **Sunflower Parmesan "Cheese"** !

1½ cups cooked black beans (see here)
1½ cups cooked red kidney beans (see here)
1 cup cooked brown rice (see here)
1 cup quick-cooking oats
¼ cup Easy One-Pot Vegan Marinara
1 tablespoon Italian seasoning
1 teaspoon garlic powder
1 teaspoon onion powder
¼ teaspoon freshly ground black pepper

1. Preheat the oven to 400°F. Line a baking sheet with parchment paper.
2. In a large bowl, use a fork or mixing spoon to mash the black beans and kidney beans together.
3. Add the rice, oats, marinara, Italian seasoning, garlic powder, onion powder, and pepper. Stir until well combined.
4. Scoop out ¼ cup of the bean mixture, and form into a ball. Place the bean ball on the baking sheet. Repeat with the remaining bean mixture.

5. Bake the bean balls for 30 minutes, or until lightly browned and heated through, turning them once after about 15 minutes.

MAKE-AHEAD TIP: You can prepare these bean balls ahead of time, and freeze them to have on hand as a ready-to-heat snack.

PER SERVING
Calories: 144; Total fat: 2g; Carbohydrates: 26g; Fiber: 5g; Protein: 6g

Crispy Rice-and-Bean Tostadas

SERVES 2

1 POT, 5 INGREDIENTS, 30 MINUTES, GLUTEN FREE, NUT FREE • PREP TIME: 10 MINUTES • COOK TIME: 10 MINUTES

Tostadas are flat, toasted tortillas that can be topped with your favorite Mexican ingredients and seasonings. If you keep precooked staples like rice and beans in your refrigerator, this recipe will be a snap to make. It's also a great option for picky eaters, because they can choose their own favorite toppings.

4 corn tortillas
1 cup Fat-Free Refried Beans
1 cup cooked brown rice (see here)
1 cup cooked black beans (see here)
1 lime, quartered

1. Preheat the oven to 400°F. Line a baking sheet with parchment paper.
2. Place the tortillas on the baking sheet, and bake for 5 to 8 minutes, or until the tortillas turn crisp and golden brown. (Make sure to keep a close eye on them, as they can burn quickly if left in for too long.)
3. Evenly spread ¼ cup of refried beans onto each crispy tortilla, then add ¼ cup each of rice and black beans.
4. Squeeze lime juice over each tostada right before serving.

SERVING TIP: These tostadas are great on their own, but you can elevate them with toppings such as Plant-Powered "Sour Cream" , Roasted Jalapeño and Lime Guacamole , fresh cilantro and corn, salsa, and hot sauce.

PER SERVING
Calories: 422; Total fat: 4g; Carbohydrates: 81g; Fiber: 19g; Protein: 19g

Southwest Stuffed Peppers

SERVES 4

GLUTEN FREE, NUT FREE • PREP TIME: 10 MINUTES • COOK TIME: 30 MINUTES

Stuffed peppers are great if you're looking for a delicious, easy dinner that also stores well for leftovers. Red or yellow bell peppers will impart a bit more flavor to the dish. To kick the heat up, add a few slices of jalapeño into the rice mixture before filling the bell peppers.

4 bell peppers
3 cups cooked brown rice (see here)
1 cup cooked black beans (see here)
1 cup corn (fresh or frozen)
1 cup vegetable broth
2 tablespoons tomato paste
2 tablespoons chili powder
1 teaspoon ground cumin

1. Preheat the oven to 375°F.
2. Cut the tops off the bell peppers, and remove any seeds or fibers that remain inside the core or inside the tops of the peppers.
3. In a large bowl, mix together the rice, beans, corn, broth, tomato paste, chili powder, and cumin until the tomato paste and spices have been thoroughly incorporated.
4. Spoon one-quarter of the rice mixture into each pepper. Set the peppers upright on a baking dish, and place the tops back onto the peppers.
5. Bake for 1 hour, or until the peppers are easily pierced with a fork, and serve.

TECHNIQUE TIP: To reduce the baking time, complete the instructions through step 2, then place the peppers in a pot of boiling water for 5 minutes or microwave them for 1 minute. Proceed with steps 3 and 4, then bake for 30 minutes.

PER SERVING
Calories: 270; Total fat: 3g; Carbohydrates: 55g; Fiber: 9g; Protein: 11g

Easy Enchilada Bake

SERVES 6

GLUTEN FREE, NUT FREE • PREP TIME: 10 MINUTES • COOK TIME: 30 MINUTES

Enchilada bakes make a great dish to bring to a potluck or family get-together. This one's also great if you want to make a double or triple batch and then portion it out for lunches and dinners throughout the week. You can also prepare this recipe a day or two ahead of time, and store it in the refrigerator until you're ready to bake it.

FOR THE ENCHILADA SAUCE

2½ cups water
¼ cup tomato paste
2 tablespoons chili powder
1 teaspoon paprika
1 teaspoon garlic powder
1 teaspoon onion powder
1 teaspoon ground cumin

FOR THE ENCHILADA BAKE

2 cups cooked brown rice (see here)
2 cups cooked black beans (see here)
1 cup corn (fresh or frozen)
8 corn tortillas
½ cup Fat-Free Refried Beans (here) or mashed pinto beans

TO MAKE THE ENCHILADA SAUCE

In a blender, blend the water, tomato paste, chili powder, paprika, garlic powder, onion powder, and cumin for 1 to 2 minutes, or until thoroughly blended.

TO MAKE THE ENCHILADA BAKE

1. Preheat the oven to 375°F.

2. Reserve ½ cup of enchilada sauce, and set aside.
3. In a large bowl, mix together the rice, black beans, corn, and the remaining enchilada sauce.
4. Cover the bottom of a baking dish with 4 corn tortillas, then evenly spread the refried beans over the tortillas.
5. Top the refried beans with an even layer of the rice mixture.
6. Place the remaining 4 tortillas on top of the filling. Spread the reserved ½ cup of enchilada sauce over the tortillas, making sure they are covered with the sauce.
7. Place the enchiladas in the oven and bake for 30 minutes, or until lightly browned. Serve warm.

VARIATION TIP: Enchilada bakes can be customized in a number of ways. Try adding young green jackfruit to make it a "shredded chicken" enchilada bake, or toss in some of your favorite seasonal vegetables to keep it fresh and exciting.

PER SERVING
Calories: 259; Total fat: 3g; Carbohydrates: 51g; Fiber: 11g; Protein: 11g

Burrito Bowl with Oil-Free Tortilla Chips

SERVES 2

30 MINUTES, GLUTEN FREE, NUT FREE • PREP TIME: 10 MINUTES • COOK TIME: 10 MINUTES

Burrito bowls are a great option when you have a refrigerator and pantry full of cooked or ready-to-heat staples. With the addition of a few spices, this burrito bowl may become your new lunchtime favorite. This recipe can also be prepared ahead of time and then frozen for up to 3 months, for future lunches or dinners.

4 corn tortillas
1 cup cooked brown rice (see <u>here</u>)
1 cup cooked black beans (see <u>here</u>)
1 cup corn (fresh or frozen)
2 teaspoons chili powder
1 teaspoon ground cumin
½ teaspoon garlic powder
½ teaspoon onion powder
2 cups shredded lettuce
1 avocado, peeled, pitted, and sliced ¼ cup salsa

1. Preheat the oven to 350°F. Line a baking sheet with parchment paper.
2. Cut each tortilla into 6 evenly-sized chips, and place the chips on the baking sheet. Bake for 8 to 10 minutes, or until golden brown. The chips will continue to crisp up as they cool.
3. In a large bowl, combine the rice, black beans, corn, chili powder, cumin, garlic powder, and onion powder. If the rice and beans are cold, warm this mixture in the microwave on

high for 2 minutes or on the stovetop in a medium saucepan over medium heat for 5 minutes.
4. Divide the warm rice, bean, and corn mixture into two serving bowls, then top each bowl with 1 cup of shredded lettuce and half of the avocado slices and salsa.
5. Serve with the crispy tortilla chips and any other WFPB condiment of your choosing.

SERVING TIP: Burrito bowls can be made in an à la carte fashion by having all of the fillings heated and ready, allowing others to add in all of the ingredients they would prefer. This can be a great option for picky eaters who like to choose exactly what goes into their bowl.

PER SERVING
Calories: 538; Total fat: 17g; Carbohydrates: 86g; Fiber: 21g; Protein: 18g

Homestyle Lentil Loaf with Maple-Balsamic Glaze

SERVES 6

GLUTEN FREE, NUT FREE • PREP TIME: 10 MINUTES • COOK TIME: 30 MINUTES

This lentil loaf is for both fans and critics of traditional meatloaf. Full of savory seasonings and hearty starchy staples, this lentil loaf will steal the show at your next dinner party or potluck. If you're fixing this for children, allowing them to help in the preparation and add in their favorite vegetables can help get them excited about this recipe.

FOR THE GLAZE

1 tablespoon balsamic vinegar
1 tablespoon tomato paste
½ tablespoon maple syrup

FOR THE LENTIL LOAF

2 cups cooked brown or green lentils (see here)
1 cup quick-cooking oats
1 cup cooked brown rice (see here)
¼ cup vegetable broth
¼ cup Sweet and Tangy Ketchup
2 tablespoons nutritional yeast
2 teaspoons onion powder
1 teaspoon garlic powder
1 teaspoon dried sage ½
teaspoon dried thyme
½ teaspoon freshly ground black pepper ½ teaspoon baking powder

TO MAKE THE GLAZE

In a small bowl, whisk together the vinegar, tomato paste, and maple syrup.

TO MAKE THE LENTIL LOAF

1. Preheat the oven to 400°F.
2. In a large bowl, combine the lentils, oats, rice, broth, ketchup, nutritional yeast, onion powder, garlic powder, sage, thyme, pepper, and baking powder. Mix together until the spices and oats have been thoroughly mixed and the lentils mashed. Transfer the mixture into a nonstick bread pan or a baking dish lined with parchment paper.
3. Brush the glaze evenly over the top of the loaf before placing in the oven.
4. Bake for 30 minutes, or until lightly browned, and serve.

SERVING TIP: Leftover lentil loaf added to a bowl of Fluffy Mashed Potatoes with Gravy or served on a few slices of whole-grain bread is a surefire lunchtime winner.

PER SERVING
Calories: 197; Total fat: 2g; Carbohydrates: 36g; Fiber: 9g; Protein: 12g

Lucky Mint Smoothie

CHAPTER 6
Smoothies and Beverages

Smoothies and other WFPB beverages can be great ways to start the morning or a refreshing way to cool off on warm summer days. With a handful of simple ingredients, you can make plant-based milks, smoothies, and cold drinks in just a few minutes. Many of these recipes can be made ahead of time and enjoyed over the course of a few days or all at once. Whether you're into green smoothies or warm lattes, you can sip happily knowing that your beverages are in line with your dietary and health goals.

Watermelon Limenade
Bubbly Orange Soda
Creamy Cashew Milk
Homemade Oat Milk
Lucky Mint Smoothie
Paradise Island Smoothie
Apple Pie Smoothie
Peanut Butter and Chia Smoothie
Lean Green Chocolate Smoothie
Lemon-Ginger Tea

Cold-Brew Peach Iced Tea

Maple-Cinnamon Latte

Watermelon Limenade

SERVES 6

5 INGREDIENTS, 30 MINUTES, GLUTEN FREE, NUT FREE • PREP TIME: 5 MINUTES

When it comes to refreshing summertime drinks, lemonade is always near the top of the list. This Watermelon "Limenade" is perfect for using up leftover watermelon or for those early fall days when stores and farmers are almost giving them away. You can also substitute 4 cups of ice for the cold water to create a delicious summertime slushy.

4 cups diced watermelon
4 cups cold water
2 tablespoons freshly squeezed lemon juice
1 tablespoon freshly squeezed lime juice

1. In a blender, combine the watermelon, water, lemon juice, and lime juice, and blend for 1 minute.
2. Strain the contents through a fine-mesh sieve or nut-milk bag. Serve chilled. Store in the refrigerator for up to 3 days.

SERVING TIP: Slice up a few lemon or lime wedges to serve with your Watermelon Limenade, or top it with a few fresh mint leaves to give it an extra-crisp, minty flavor.

PER SERVING
Calories: 60; Total fat: 0g; Carbohydrates: 15g; Fiber: 1g; Protein: 1g

Bubbly Orange Soda

SERVES 4

5 INGREDIENTS, 30 MINUTES, GLUTEN FREE, NUT FREE • PREP TIME: 5 MINUTES

Soda can be one of the toughest things to give up when you first adopt a WFPB diet. That's partially because refined sugars and caffeine are addictive, but it can also be because carbonated beverages are fun to drink! With sweetness from the orange juice and bubbliness from the carbonated water, this orange "soda" is perfect for assisting in the transition from SAD to WFPB.

4 cups carbonated water

2 cups pulp-free orange juice (4 oranges, freshly squeezed and strained)

For each serving, pour 2 parts carbonated water and 1 part orange juice over ice right before serving. Stir and enjoy.

SERVING TIP: This recipe is best made right before drinking. The amount of fizz in the carbonated water will decrease the longer it's open, so if you're going to make it ahead of time, make sure it's stored in an airtight, refrigerator-safe container.

PER SERVING
Calories: 56; Total fat: 0g; Carbohydrates: 13g; Fiber: 0g; Protein: 1g

Creamy Cashew Milk

SERVES 8

5 INGREDIENTS, GLUTEN FREE • PREP TIME: 5 MINUTES, PLUS OVERNIGHT TO SOAK

Learning how to make your own plant-based milks can be one of the best ways to save money and ditch dairy for good. This is one of the easiest milk recipes to master, and if you have a high-speed blender, you can skip the straining step and go straight to a refrigerator-safe container. Large mason jars work great for storing plant-based milk, as they allow you to give a quick shake before each use.

4 cups water
¼ cup raw cashews, soaked overnight

1. In a blender, blend the water and cashews on high speed for 2 minutes.
2. Strain with a nut-milk bag or cheesecloth, then store in the refrigerator for up to 5 days.

VARIATION TIP: This recipe makes unsweetened cashew milk that can be used in savory and sweet dishes. For a creamier version to put in your coffee, cut the amount of water in half. For a sweeter version, add 1 to 2 tablespoons maple syrup and 1 teaspoon vanilla extract before blending.

PER SERVING
Calories: 18; Total fat: 2g; Carbohydrates: 1g; Fiber: 0g; Protein: 1g

Homemade Oat Milk

SERVES 8

5 INGREDIENTS, 30 MINUTES, GLUTEN FREE, NUT FREE • PREP TIME: 5 MINUTES, PLUS 15 MINUTES TO SOAK

Oat milk is a fantastic option if you need a nut-free milk or just want an extremely inexpensive plant-based milk. Making a half-gallon jar at home costs a fraction of the price of other plant-based or dairy milks. Oat milk can be used in both savory and sweet dishes.

1 cup rolled oats
4 cups water

1. Put the oats in a medium bowl, and cover with cold water. Soak for 15 minutes, then drain and rinse the oats.
2. Pour the cold water and the soaked oats into a blender. Blend for 60 to 90 seconds, or just until the mixture is a creamy white color throughout. (Blending any further may overblend the oats, resulting in a gummy milk.)
3. Strain through a nut-milk bag or colander, then store in the refrigerator for up to 5 days.

VARIATION TIP: This recipe can easily be made into chocolate oat milk. Once you've strained the oat milk, return it to a blender with 3 tablespoons cocoa powder, 2 tablespoons maple syrup, and 1 teaspoon vanilla extract, then blend for 30 seconds.

PER SERVING
Calories: 39; Total fat: 1g; Carbohydrates: 7g; Fiber: 1g; Protein: 1g

Lucky Mint Smoothie

SERVES 2

5 INGREDIENTS, 30 MINUTES, GLUTEN FREE, NUT FREE • PREP TIME: 5 MINUTES

As spring approaches and mint begins to once again take over the garden, "Irish"-themed green shakes begin to pop up as well. In contrast to the traditionally high-fat, sugary shakes, this smoothie is a wonderful option for sunny spring days. So next time you want to sip on something cool and minty, do so with a health-promoting Lucky Mint Smoothie.

2 cups plant-based milk (here or here)
2 frozen bananas, halved
1 tablespoon fresh mint leaves or ¼ teaspoon peppermint extract
1 teaspoon vanilla extract

In a blender, combine the milk, bananas, mint, and vanilla. Blend on high for 1 to 2 minutes, or until the contents reach a smooth and creamy consistency, and serve.

VARIATION TIP: If you like to sneak greens into smoothies, add a cup or two of spinach to boost the health benefits of this smoothie and give it an even greener appearance.

PER SERVING
Calories: 152; Total fat: 4g; Carbohydrates: 30g; Fiber: 4g; Protein: 2g

Paradise Island Smoothie

SERVES 2

5 INGREDIENTS, 30 MINUTES, GLUTEN FREE, NUT FREE • PREP TIME: 5 MINUTES

While taking a trip to a tropical paradise may not be on your current schedule, making this simple and delicious smoothie definitely can be. And since most grocery stores carry pineapple and mango chunks in their frozen fruits section, prepping for this recipe is an island breeze.

2 cups plant-based milk (here or here)
1 frozen banana
½ cup frozen mango chunks
½ cup frozen pineapple chunks
1 teaspoon vanilla extract

In a blender, combine the milk, banana, mango, pineapple, and vanilla. Blend on high for 1 to 2 minutes, or until the contents reach a smooth and creamy consistency, and serve.

LEFTOVER TIP: If you have any leftover smoothie, you can put it in a jar with some rolled oats and allow the mixture to soak in the refrigerator overnight to create a tropical version of overnight oats.

PER SERVING
Calories: 176; Total fat: 4g; Carbohydrates: 36g; Fiber: 4g; Protein: 2g

Apple Pie Smoothie

SERVES 2

30 MINUTES, GLUTEN FREE, NUT FREE • PREP TIME: 5 MINUTES

This smoothie is great for a quick breakfast or a cool dessert. Its combination of sweet apples and warming cinnamon is sure to win over children and adults alike. If the holidays find you in a warm area, this smoothie may just be the cool treat you've been looking for to take the place of pie at dessert time.

2 sweet crisp apples, cut into 1-inch cubes
2 cups plant-based milk (here or here)
1 cup ice
1 tablespoon maple syrup
1 teaspoon ground cinnamon
1 teaspoon vanilla extract

In a blender, combine the apples, milk, ice, maple syrup, cinnamon, and vanilla. Blend on high for 1 to 2 minutes, or until the contents reach a smooth and creamy consistency, and serve.

VARIATION TIP: You can also use this recipe for making overnight oatmeal. Blend your smoothie, mix it with 2 cups rolled oats, and refrigerate overnight for a premade breakfast for two.

PER SERVING
Calories: 198; Total fat: 6g; Carbohydrates: 32g; Fiber: 8g; Protein: 3g

Peanut Butter and Chia Smoothie

SERVES 2

5 INGREDIENTS, 30 MINUTES, GLUTEN FREE • PREP TIME: 5 MINUTES

Smoothies are wonderful because you can have them for breakfast, lunch, a snack, or dessert. This one makes a great morning meal on those days when you need something ready in just a few minutes. If you're out of plant-based milks, you can substitute water and add an extra ½ tablespoon of peanut powder and still have a great-tasting smoothie.

3 frozen bananas, halved
1 cup plant-based milk (here or here)
2 tablespoons defatted peanut powder
1 teaspoon vanilla extract
½ tablespoon chia seeds

1. In a blender or food processor, combine the bananas, milk, peanut powder, and vanilla. Blend on high for 1 to 2 minutes.
2. Add the chia seeds, and pulse 2 to 4 times, or until the chia seeds have dispersed evenly without being blended up, and serve.

SUBSTITUTION TIP: If you're allergic to peanuts, you can use various other defatted nut powders, such as almond powder. And if you'd prefer to use peanut butter, substitute 2 tablespoons for the powder.

PER SERVING
Calories: 271; Total fat: 5g; Carbohydrates: 47g; Fiber: 8g; Protein: 11g

Lean Green Chocolate Smoothie

SERVES 2

5 INGREDIENTS, 30 MINUTES, GLUTEN FREE, NUT FREE • PREP TIME: 5 MINUTES

In many ways, smoothies can be great for sneaking extra vegetables into your family's diet. But this lean green smoothie goes a step further and makes your favorite leafy greens the star. Make sure you use extremely ripe frozen bananas in order to maximize their sweetness and balance out any bitterness from the greens.

6 ounces greens (kale, collards, or spinach)
2 very ripe frozen bananas, halved
3 cups plant-based milk (here or here)
2 tablespoons cocoa powder
1 teaspoon vanilla extract

In a blender, combine the greens, bananas, milk, cocoa powder, and vanilla. Blend on high for 1 to 2 minutes, or until the contents reach a smooth and creamy consistency, and serve.

PER SERVING
Calories: 225; Total fat: 6g; Carbohydrates: 42g; Fiber: 8g; Protein: 6g

Lemon-Ginger Tea

SERVES 2

5 INGREDIENTS, 30 MINUTES, GLUTEN FREE, NUT FREE • PREP TIME: 5 MINUTES • COOK TIME: 15 MINUTES

Herbal teas have many applications, but chief among them may be to help warm you up in the morning before starting the day. Not only do ginger and lemon have many health benefits, but also they add a ton a flavor to this tasty tea. Feel free to change the ratios of ginger, lemon, and maple syrup to suit your taste.

4 cups water
2 tablespoons freshly squeezed lemon juice
1 tablespoon minced ginger
1 tablespoon maple syrup

1. In a medium saucepan, bring the water to a boil. Remove from the heat and stir in the lemon juice, ginger, and maple syrup. Cover, and steep for 15 minutes.
2. Strain through a sieve and enjoy hot, or let cool and pour over a glass filled with ice to enjoy as a cold drink.

MAKE-AHEAD TIP: This recipe can be made ahead of time and then chilled in the refrigerator so you can have a tasty herbal iced tea any time of the day.

PER SERVING
Calories: 39; Total fat: 0g; Carbohydrates: 9g; Fiber: 0g; Protein: 0g

Cold-Brew Peach Iced Tea

SERVES 6

5 INGREDIENTS, GLUTEN FREE, NUT FREE • PREP TIME: 10 MINUTES, PLUS 8 HOURS OR OVERNIGHT TO STEEP

Nothing is quite as thirst-quenching on a hot summer day as iced tea, but homemade iced teas often turn out overly bitter. By cold-brewing this peach iced tea, you'll be able to avoid the bitterness created by tannins released during the traditional process of steeping the tea bags in hot water.

4 ripe peaches, sliced
8 cups water
5 tea bags (black, green, or white)

In a pitcher, combine the peach slices, water, and tea bags. Place in the refrigerator, and allow to steep overnight (8 to 12 hours). Store in the refrigerator for up to 5 days.

SUBSTITUTION TIP: Mix it up with fresh berries, mint, or ginger to create more types of refreshing iced tea. Also feel free to add or subtract the number of tea bags to make this recipe stronger or weaker.

PER SERVING
Calories: 39; Total fat: 0g; Carbohydrates: 9g; Fiber: 2g; Protein: 1g

Maple-Cinnamon Latte

SERVES 2

5 INGREDIENTS, 30 MINUTES, GLUTEN FREE, NUT FREE • PREP TIME: 5 MINUTES • COOK TIME: 10 MINUTES

A great thing about adopting a WFPB diet is that you really don't have to give up many of the things you already enjoy. With a few simple changes, your favorite drinks or recipes can be transformed into much healthier versions. This Maple-Cinnamon Latte is a perfect example of making a few simple changes to create a warm and delicious morning drink.

3 cups plant-based milk (here or here)
1 tablespoon maple syrup
1 teaspoon ground cinnamon

1. In a medium saucepan on the stovetop, heat the milk until it just begins to boil, or microwave in a microwave-safe bowl on high for 2 minutes.
2. Pour the warmed milk, maple syrup, and cinnamon into a blender, and blend for 1 to 2 minutes, or until the mixture turns frothy. Serve warm.

SUBSTITUTION TIP: For a caffeinated latte, substitute ½ cup strongly brewed coffee for ½ cup milk.

PER SERVING
Calories: 89; Total fat: 5g; Carbohydrates: 11g; Fiber: 2g; Protein: 2g

Chocolate-Peppermint Nice Cream

CHAPTER 7
Snacks and Desserts

Traditionally, snacks and desserts contain large amounts of salt, oil, and sugar. But the recipes to follow will show you that this doesn't have to be the case. On a WFPB diet, snacks can play a crucial role in helping curb any midday hunger that might arise at work or at home. Desserts, which you may previously have kept aside for only special occasions, can now be enjoyed regularly as WFPB staples. Beyond the recipes provided, fresh fruits and vegetables are always a great option for easy and delicious desserts and snack foods.

[Kale Chips](#)
[Showtime Popcorn](#)
[Strawberry-Avocado Toast with Balsamic Glaze](#)
[Strawberry-Watermelon Ice Pops](#)
[Chocolate-Peppermint Nice Cream](#)
[Peanut Butter Nice Cream](#)
[Sweet Potato Pie Nice Cream](#)
[Oat Crunch Apple Crisp](#)
[Sweet Potato Spice Cake](#)
[Chocolate Microwave Mug Cake](#)

Kale Chips

SERVES 4

5 INGREDIENTS, 30 MINUTES, GLUTEN FREE, NUT FREE • PREP TIME: 5 MINUTES • COOK TIME: 20 MINUTES

Crunchy snacks are one of the big things that some people miss when they first begin eating a WFPB diet. An easy-to-make and nutritious snack that can help with your cravings is Kale Chips. These can be made in large or small batches and store extremely well in airtight containers for up to 2 months.

¼ cup vegetable broth
1 tablespoon nutritional yeast
½ teaspoon garlic powder
½ teaspoon onion powder
6 ounces kale, stemmed and cut into 2- to 3-inch pieces

1. Preheat the oven to 300°F. Line a baking sheet with parchment paper.
2. In a small bowl, mix together the broth, nutritional yeast, garlic powder, and onion powder.
3. Put the kale in a large bowl. Pour the broth and seasonings over the kale, and toss well to thoroughly coat.
4. Place the kale pieces on the baking sheet in an even layer. Bake for 20 minutes, or until crispy, turning the kale halfway through.

VARIATION TIP: For a smoky flavor, add a teaspoon of smoked paprika to the recipe. To create spicy kale chips, add ½ teaspoon red pepper flakes.

PER SERVING
Calories: 41; Total fat: 0g; Carbohydrates: 7g; Fiber: 2g; Protein: 4g

Showtime Popcorn

SERVES 2

5 INGREDIENTS, 30 MINUTES, GLUTEN FREE, NUT FREE • PREP TIME: 1 MINUTE • COOK TIME: 5 MINUTES

This is a fantastic alternative to microwave popcorns full of oil and salt. Once you get the hang of popping your own popcorn, you can get creative finding different flavors and seasonings that fit your preferences. If you don't have a microwave, air poppers are great for making oil-free popcorn in just a few minutes.

¼ **cup popcorn kernels**
1 tablespoon nutritional yeast
¼ **teaspoon garlic powder**
¼ **teaspoon onion powder**

1. Put the popcorn kernels in a paper lunch bag, folding over the top of the bag so the kernels won't spill out.
2. Microwave on high for 2 to 3 minutes, or until you hear a pause of 2 seconds in between kernels popping.
3. Remove the bag from the microwave, and add the nutritional yeast, garlic powder, and onion powder. Fold the top of the bag back over, and shake to thoroughly coat.
4. Pour into a bowl and enjoy.

PER SERVING
Calories: 48; Total fat: 1g; Carbohydrates: 6g; Fiber: 2g; Protein: 4g

Strawberry-Avocado Toast with Balsamic Glaze

SERVES 4

5 INGREDIENTS, 30 MINUTES, NUT FREE • PREP TIME: 5 MINUTES

When it comes to speedy breakfasts, toast is a mainstay. But this recipe isn't just for any old toast—this is toast taken to another level. The avocado adds creaminess, the sliced strawberry brings a fresh fruitiness, and the balsamic glaze rounds out the flavors with a hint of acidity and sweetness.

1 avocado, peeled, pitted, and quartered
4 whole-wheat bread slices, toasted
4 ripe strawberries, cut into ¼-inch slices
1 tablespoon balsamic glaze or reduction

Mash one-quarter of the avocado on a slice of toast. Layer one-quarter of the strawberry slices over the avocado, and finish with a drizzle of balsamic glaze. Repeat with the remaining ingredients, and serve.

INGREDIENT TIP: If you can't buy balsamic glaze, make your own! Put balsamic vinegar in a small saucepan and cook, uncovered, over low heat for roughly 45 minutes, or until it's reduced to roughly one-quarter of the original amount of liquid.

PER SERVING
Calories: 150; Total fat: 8g; Carbohydrates: 17g; Fiber: 5g; Protein: 5g

Strawberry-Watermelon Ice Pops

SERVES 6

5 INGREDIENTS, GLUTEN FREE, NUT FREE • PREP TIME: 5 MINUTES, PLUS AT LEAST 6 HOURS TO FREEZE

These ice pops make a great treat on hot summer days or when that late-night sweet tooth is calling. They're simple to make and can be adjusted in many ways to meet your family's personal preferences. Feel free to get creative with other types of melons and fruits to make this recipe your own.

4 cups diced watermelon
4 strawberries, tops removed
2 tablespoons freshly squeezed lime juice

1. In a blender, combine the watermelon, strawberries, and lime juice. Blend for 1 to 2 minutes, or until well combined.
2. Pour evenly into 6 ice-pop molds, insert ice-pop sticks, and freeze for at least 6 hours before serving.

PREPARATION TIP: Silicone or stainless steel ice-pop molds can be purchased online or at some specialty grocery stores. Or you can always use paper cups and ice-pop sticks to make this frozen treat.

PER SERVING
Calories: 61; Total fat: 0g; Carbohydrates: 15g; Fiber: 1g; Protein: 1g

Chocolate-Peppermint Nice Cream

SERVES 2

5 INGREDIENTS, 30 MINUTES, GLUTEN FREE, NUT FREE • PREP TIME: 5 MINUTES

Keeping some bananas ready to go in your freezer is always a good idea. A helpful tip for nice creams is to make sure that the bananas are well ripened before peeling and freezing them. Chocolate and peppermint are a perfect combination for an after-dinner treat or midday snack on a warm summer day.

3 frozen ripe bananas, broken into thirds
3 tablespoons plant-based milk (here or here)
2 tablespoons cocoa powder
⅛ teaspoon peppermint extract

1. In a food processor, combine the bananas, milk, cocoa powder, and peppermint.
2. Process on medium speed for 30 to 60 seconds, or until the bananas have been blended into smooth soft-serve consistency, and serve. (If you notice any banana pieces stuck toward the top and sides of the food processor, you may need to stop and scrape them down with a spatula, then pulse until smooth.)

TECHNIQUE TIP: If you don't have a food processor, blenders work, too. For high-speed blenders, use the tamper tool to ensure all banana gets blended properly. For less powerful blenders, use ¼ to ½ cup plant-based milk instead of 2 tablespoons.

PER SERVING
Calories: 173; Total fat: 2g; Carbohydrates: 43g; Fiber: 6g; Protein: 3g

Peanut Butter Nice Cream

SERVES 2

5 INGREDIENTS, 30 MINUTES, GLUTEN FREE • PREP TIME: 5 MINUTES

High-fat, sugar-filled ice cream is a late-night staple in many households. Luckily, there are easy, healthy WFPB versions like this Peanut Butter Nice Cream. Defatted peanut powder is a great option for making nice creams that are lower in fat while still containing the great flavor of peanut butter.

3 frozen ripe bananas, broken into thirds
3 tablespoons plant-based milk (here or here)
2 tablespoons defatted peanut powder
1 teaspoon vanilla extract

1. In a food processor, combine the bananas, milk, peanut powder, and vanilla.
2. Process on medium speed for 30 to 60 seconds, or until the bananas have been blended into a smooth soft-serve consistency, and serve. (If you notice any banana pieces stuck toward the top and sides of the food processor, you may need to stop and scrape them down with a spatula, then pulse until smooth.)

SUBSTITUTION TIP: You can swap out bananas for many different types of frozen fruits, including mango, peach, or pineapple.

PER SERVING
Calories: 237; Total fat: 3g; Carbohydrates: 45g; Fiber: 7g; Protein: 10g

Sweet Potato Pie Nice Cream

SERVES 2

5 INGREDIENTS, GLUTEN FREE • PREP TIME: 5 MINUTES, PLUS AT LEAST 4 HOURS TO FREEZE

The common fruit for making many nice creams is bananas, but there are many other options to use as a base for these tasty frozen treats. One option is to use sweet potatoes that have been cooked and then frozen. This sweet treat can be made at any time of the year but is definitely a favorite in the fall.

2 medium sweet potatoes, cooked (see here)
½ cup plant-based milk (here or here)
1 tablespoon maple syrup
1 teaspoon vanilla extract
½ teaspoon ground cinnamon

1. Line a baking sheet with parchment paper.
2. Remove the skin from the cooked sweet potatoes, and cut the flesh into 1-inch cubes. Place on the baking sheet in an even layer, then place in the freezer overnight, or for a minimum of 4 hours.
3. In a food processor, combine the frozen sweet potato, milk, maple syrup, vanilla, and cinnamon.
4. Process on medium speed for 1 to 2 minutes, or until the mixture has been blended into a smooth soft-serve consistency, and serve. (If you notice any sweet potato pieces stuck toward the top and sides of the food processor, you may need to stop and scrape them down with a spatula, then pulse until smooth.)

SERVING TIP: Nice cream is the perfect dessert to enjoy all by itself, but it also goes great with other WFPB desserts. A scoop of nice cream on top of a Chocolate Microwave Mug Cake or Sweet Potato Spice Cake can elevate them to new heights!

PER SERVING
Calories: 155; Total fat: 1g; Carbohydrates: 34g; Fiber: 5g; Protein: 2g

Oat Crunch Apple Crisp

SERVES 6

GLUTEN FREE, NUT FREE • PREP TIME: 10 MINUTES • COOK TIME: 35 MINUTES

Apples and fall go together almost as well as cinnamon and fall, so why not enjoy both in one dish? Sweet crisp apples stay a bit firmer and provide some bite, but feel free to use whatever apples are locally available. This is a great dish to bring to a holiday party or potluck.

3 medium apples, cored and cut into ¼-inch pieces ¾ cup apple juice
1 teaspoon vanilla extract
1 teaspoon ground cinnamon, divided
2 cups rolled oats
¼ cup maple syrup

1. Preheat the oven to 375°F.
2. In a large bowl, combine the apple slices, apple juice, vanilla, and ½ teaspoon of cinnamon. Mix well to thoroughly coat the apple slices.
3. Layer the apple slices on the bottom of a round or square baking dish. Take any leftover liquid and pour it over the apple slices.
4. In a large bowl, stir together the oats, maple syrup, and the remaining ½ teaspoon of cinnamon until the oats are completely coated.
5. Sprinkle the oat mixture over the apples, being sure to spread it out evenly so that none of the apple slices are visible.
6. Bake for 35 minutes, or until the oats begin to turn golden brown, and serve.

PER SERVING
Calories: 213; Total fat: 2g; Carbohydrates: 47g; Fiber: 6g; Protein: 4g

Sweet Potato Spice Cake

SERVES 6

NUT FREE • PREP TIME: 5 MINUTES • COOK TIME: 45 MINUTES

If you're looking for the perfect dessert that can be prepped in just a few minutes, look no further than this delicious cake. It's full of warming spices and just enough sweetness to make it a perfect dessert for dinner or teatime. The sweet potato used in this recipe can be cooked in any of the ways mentioned **here**, but remember: the softer and sweeter, the better.

1 sweet potato, cooked and peeled (see here)
½ cup unsweetened applesauce
½ cup plant-based milk (here or here) ¼ cup maple syrup
1 teaspoon vanilla extract
2 cups whole-wheat flour
½ teaspoon baking soda
½ teaspoon ground cinnamon
¼ teaspoon ground ginger

1. Preheat the oven to 350°F.
2. In a large mixing bowl, use a fork or potato masher to mash the sweet potato.
3. Mix in the applesauce, milk, maple syrup, and vanilla.
4. Stir in the flour, baking soda, cinnamon, and ginger until the dry ingredients have been thoroughly combined with the wet ingredients.
5. Pour the batter into a nonstick baking dish or one lined with parchment paper. Bake for 45 minutes, or until you can stick a knife into the middle of the cake and it comes out clean.

6. Cool, slice, and serve.

SERVING TIP: This cake pairs great with a scoop or two of Peanut Butter Nice Cream or Sweet Potato Pie Nice Cream .

PER SERVING
Calories: 238; Total fat: 1g; Carbohydrates: 52g; Fiber: 2g; Protein: 5g

Chocolate Microwave Mug Cake

SERVES 1

1 POT, 30 MINUTES, NUT FREE • PREP TIME: 5 MINUTES • COOK TIME: 90 SECONDS, PLUS 5 MINUTES TO COOL

With the help of a microwave, you're never more than a few minutes away from a mug full of chocolaty goodness. Mug cakes can be made in microwave-safe bowls or cups, but the best results happen in a coffee mug. Just make sure to fill the mug no more than three-quarters of the way full before cooking to allow room for the cake to rise.

3 tablespoons whole-wheat flour
3 tablespoons unsweetened applesauce
1 tablespoon cocoa powder
1 tablespoon maple syrup
1 tablespoon plant-based milk (here or here)
1 teaspoon vanilla extract
¼ teaspoon baking powder

1. In a microwave-safe coffee mug or bowl, combine the flour, applesauce, cocoa powder, maple syrup, milk, vanilla, and baking powder. Stir together until there are no clumps of dry flour left. (Place the mug on a paper towel or plate to ensure easy cleanup.)
2. Microwave on high for 90 seconds, or until the cake has risen to the top of the mug.
3. Remove from the microwave and set aside to cool for a minimum of 5 minutes before serving.

ALTERNATE PREPARATION: Chocolate mug cake can be easily baked if you do not have a microwave or would just prefer to use the oven. Follow step 1 and then bake for 25 to 30 minutes at 350°F.

PER SERVING
Calories: 185; Total fat: 1g; Carbohydrates: 41g; Fiber: 3g; Protein: 4g

Roasted Jalapeño and Lime Guacamole

CHAPTER 8
Sauces, Dressings, and Dips

It can be challenging to find sauces, dressings, and dips that are WFPB-friendly and not full of salt, oil, and sugar. You may be able to find some versions that exclude one or two of the SOSs, but your best bet for health-promoting condiments is to make them yourself. Many of these recipes can be made with simple ingredients that you might already have stocked in your pantry. Once you try them out and find the ones you really enjoy, make them regularly to keep on hand.

Sweet and Tangy Ketchup (with BBQ Sauce Option)
Easy One-Pot Vegan Marinara
Sunflower Parmesan "Cheese"
Anytime "Cheese" Sauce (with Queso Option)
Plant-Powered "Sour Cream" (with Ranch Option)
Strawberry-Peach Vinaigrette
Lemon and Poppy Seed Dressing
Roasted Garlic Dressing
Roasted Jalapeño and Lime Guacamole

White Bean and Chickpea Hummus

Sweet and Tangy Ketchup (with BBQ Sauce Option)

MAKES 2½ CUPS

1 POT, GLUTEN FREE, NUT FREE • PREP TIME: 5 MINUTES • COOK TIME: 15 MINUTES, PLUS 30 MINUTES TO COOL

Ketchup is a condiment that most people are familiar with, but unfortunately most store-bought options are filled with salt and sugar. Luckily, making your own ketchup at home is easy and takes less than 20 minutes of active cooking time. You can also use this base ketchup recipe for making a tasty WFPB BBQ sauce (see Tip).

1 cup water
1 cup tomato paste
¼ cup maple syrup
3 tablespoons apple cider vinegar
1 teaspoon garlic powder
1 teaspoon onion powder

1. In a medium saucepan, bring the water to a rolling boil over high heat. Reduce the heat to low, and whisk in the tomato paste, maple syrup, vinegar, garlic powder, and onion powder. Simmer, covered, for 10 minutes.
2. Remove from the heat and cool for about 30 minutes before transferring to a refrigerator-safe container. Store in the refrigerator for up to 1 month.

BBQ SAUCE OPTION: Transform this WFPB ketchup into a sweet and smoky BBQ sauce! After bringing the cup of water to a boil, whisk in all the ingredients for the ketchup recipe plus 2 tablespoons molasses, 1 tablespoon smoked paprika, and ½ teaspoon freshly ground black pepper. Then proceed with the instructions as listed.

PER SERVING (¼ CUP)
Calories: 45; Total fat: 0g; Carbohydrates: 11g; Fiber: 1g; Protein: 1g

Easy One-Pot Vegan Marinara

MAKES 2¼ CUPS

1 POT, 30 MINUTES, GLUTEN FREE, NUT FREE • PREP TIME: 5 MINUTES • COOK TIME: 15 MINUTES

Marinara is perfect for many different Italian-inspired WFPB recipes and meals. It goes well with the classic pairing of spaghetti and **Italian Bean Balls** while also being a great option on **Easy Vegan Pizza Bread**. Adjust the sweetness and heat by using more or less maple syrup or red pepper flakes.

1 cup water
1 cup tomato paste
2 tablespoons maple syrup
1 teaspoon dried oregano
1 teaspoon dried thyme
1 teaspoon garlic powder
1 teaspoon onion powder
½ teaspoon dried basil
¼ teaspoon red pepper flakes

1. In a medium saucepan, bring the water to a rolling boil over high heat. Reduce the heat to low, and whisk in the tomato paste, maple syrup, oregano, thyme, garlic powder, onion powder, basil, and red pepper flakes.
2. Cover and simmer for 10 minutes, stirring occasionally. Serve warm.

PREPARATION TIP: With a high-speed blender, you can forego the stovetop altogether. Blend all the ingredients for 3 to 5 minutes to get the sauce hot enough for the flavors to develop properly.

PER SERVING (½ CUP)
Calories: 69; Total fat: 0g; Carbohydrates: 17g; Fiber: 3g; Protein: 3g

Sunflower Parmesan "Cheese"

MAKES ½ CUP

5 INGREDIENTS, 30 MINUTES, GLUTEN FREE, NUT FREE • PREP TIME: 5 MINUTES

Vegan Parmesan cheese is one of the easiest recipes to make and tastes extremely similar to its animal-based counterpart. This recipe uses sunflower seeds as the base, which makes it a good option for many people with nut allergies. Sprinkle it on <u>Showtime Popcorn</u>, <u>Italian Bean Balls</u>, <u>Easy One-Pot Vegan Marinara</u>, steamed vegetables, <u>and</u> so much more!

½ cup sunflower seeds
2 tablespoons nutritional yeast
½ teaspoon garlic powder

1. In a food processor or blender, combine the sunflower seeds, nutritional yeast, and garlic powder. Process on low for 30 to 45 seconds, or until the sunflower seeds have been broken down to the size of coarse sea salt.
2. Store in a refrigerator-safe container for up to 2 months.

SUBSTITUTION TIP: You can swap in cashews or almonds for the sunflower seeds at a 1-to-1 ratio. Just make sure not to overblend, or you may end up with a Parmesan-flavored nut butter.

PER SERVING (1 TABLESPOON)
Calories: 56; Total fat: 4g; Carbohydrates: 3g; Fiber: 1g; Protein: 3g

Anytime "Cheese" Sauce (with Queso Option)

MAKES 6 CUPS

30 MINUTES, GLUTEN FREE, NUT FREE • PREP TIME: 5 MINUTES • COOK TIME: 15 MINUTES

Cheese can be one of the hardest things to give up when adopting a WFPB diet, so it's important to have healthy and delicious WFPB substitutes. Like all the recipes in this book, this one does not include salt. But if you're planning to share this recipe with friends who aren't currently SOS-free, a teaspoon or two of salt can help your cause.

1 medium Yukon Gold potato, cut into 1-inch cubes
1 medium sweet potato, cut into 1-inch cubes
¼ cup rolled oats
¼ cup nutritional yeast
1 tablespoon freshly squeezed lemon juice
2 teaspoons garlic powder
2 teaspoons onion powder
1 teaspoon smoked paprika

1. Bring a large stockpot of water to a boil over high heat. Gently and carefully immerse the Yukon Gold potato and sweet potato in the boiling water. Cook for 12 minutes. Strain, reserving 3 cups of cooking liquid.
2. In a blender, combine the reserved cooking liquid with the boiled potato and sweet potato, oats, nutritional yeast, lemon juice, garlic powder, onion powder, and paprika. Blend on high for 3 to 5 minutes, and serve.

QUESO OPTION: For a delicious WFPB queso recipe, add 1 tablespoon diced jalapeño, 2 teaspoons chili powder, and 1 teaspoon cumin before blending. Then mix in ½ cup salsa after blending.

PER SERVING (½ CUP)
Calories: 53; Total fat: 1g; Carbohydrates: 10g; Fiber: 2g; Protein: 4g

Plant-Powered "Sour Cream" (with Ranch Option)

MAKES 1 CUP

5 INGREDIENTS, 30 MINUTES, GLUTEN FREE, NUT FREE • PREP TIME: 5 MINUTES

Dairy-based sour cream or ranch may have been your go-to topping for many dishes before adopting a WFPB diet. Luckily, there are some easy plant-based versions that you may just enjoy even more than the SAD version. Adding a dollop of this plant-powered sour cream to your tacos or burrito bowls will truly do the body good.

8 ounces silken tofu
2 tablespoons freshly squeezed lemon juice
1 teaspoon apple cider vinegar
1 teaspoon onion powder

1. In a blender, combine the tofu, lemon juice, vinegar, and onion powder. Blend for 1 minute, or until the mixture reaches a creamy consistency.
2. Store in a refrigerator-safe container for up to 5 days.

RANCH OPTION: For a tasty, WFPB ranch dressing, add 1 teaspoon garlic powder, ¼ teaspoon dry dill, and ⅛ teaspoon freshly ground black pepper to the blender with the other ingredients in step 1.

PER SERVING (1 TABLESPOON)
Calories: 10; Total fat: 0g; Carbohydrates: 1g; Fiber: 0g; Protein: 1g

Strawberry-Peach Vinaigrette

MAKES 1¼ CUPS

5 INGREDIENTS, 30 MINUTES, GLUTEN FREE, NUT FREE • PREP TIME: 5 MINUTES

Summer is a great time of year to get creative with salads and dressings. Since different fruits come into season around the same time, it can be fun to test out combinations that go well with your spinach salad or spring mix. This vinaigrette is sweet and fruity while also having a touch of tartness from the balsamic vinegar.

1 peach, pitted
4 **strawberries**
¼ cup water
2 tablespoons balsamic vinegar

1. In a blender, combine the peach, strawberries, water, and vinegar. Blend on high for 1 to 2 minutes, or until the dressing has a smooth consistency.
2. Store in a refrigerator-safe container for up to 3 days.

SERVING TIP: Use this vinaigrette as a marinade for jackfruit, tofu, and tempeh before grilling. The sweetness and acidity from the dressing will help the flavors pop once these foods are cooked.

PER SERVING (2 TABLESPOONS)
Calories: 10; Total fat: 0g; Carbohydrates: 2g; Fiber: 0g; Protein: 0g

Lemon and Poppy Seed Dressing

MAKES 1 CUP

1 POT, 30 MINUTES, GLUTEN FREE, NUT FREE • PREP TIME: 5 MINUTES • COOK TIME: 10 MINUTES

This is a WFPB dressing fit for any occasion. It adds a citrus zing and a bit of sweetness that will complement all kinds of vegetables and salads. Once you give this recipe a try, you can alter the amounts of lemon juice, vinegar, and maple syrup to make it your own.

½ cup plant-based milk (here or here)
2 tablespoons freshly squeezed lemon juice
1 tablespoon apple cider vinegar
1 tablespoon maple syrup
2 teaspoons dried poppy seeds
2 teaspoons cornstarch
½ teaspoon garlic powder

1. In a small saucepan, combine the milk, lemon juice, vinegar, maple syrup, poppy seeds, cornstarch, and garlic powder. Mix until the cornstarch has completely dissolved.
2. Place the pan over medium heat and bring the dressing to a rolling boil. Whisk the dressing, then remove from the heat.
3. Allow the dressing to cool before storing in a refrigerator-safe container for up to 4 days.

SERVING TIP: If you like wilted salads, add this dressing to your greens while it's still warm. Spinach and romaine lettuce work especially well.

PER SERVING (2 TABLESPOONS)
Calories: 18; Total fat: 1g; Carbohydrates: 3g; Fiber: 0g; Protein: 0g

Roasted Garlic Dressing

MAKES 1 CUP

5 INGREDIENTS, GLUTEN FREE, NUT FREE • PREP TIME: 5 MINUTES • COOK TIME: 30 MINUTES

The key to keeping garlic from becoming bitter is to make sure that the heads roast just long enough to caramelize, becoming both sweeter and milder. You may need to roast a few extra heads of garlic, in case you start snacking on them right out of the oven.

1 head garlic
½ cup water
1 tablespoon white balsamic vinegar
1 tablespoon freshly squeezed lemon juice
1 tablespoon maple syrup

1. Preheat the oven to 400°F.
2. Remove the outermost paper-like covering from the head of garlic while still leaving the bulbs intact to the base. Slice the top of the head of garlic so that the flesh inside the bulbs is just showing.
3. Double-wrap the head of garlic in parchment paper and place it on a baking sheet. Bake for 30 minutes.
4. Remove the garlic from the oven, and unwrap the parchment paper. Squeeze the head of garlic from the base to remove the caramelized cloves. They should slide out easily.
5. In a blender, combine the caramelized garlic cloves, water, vinegar, lemon juice, and maple syrup. Blend on high for 1 minute, or until the dressing has a creamy consistency.

6. Use right away, or store in a refrigerator-safe container for up to 5 days.

PER SERVING (2 TABLESPOONS)
Calories: 13; Total fat: 0g; Carbohydrates: 3g; Fiber: 0g; Protein: 0g

Roasted Jalapeño and Lime Guacamole

SERVES 4

5 INGREDIENTS, 30 MINUTES, GLUTEN FREE, NUT FREE • PREP TIME: 5 MINUTES • COOK TIME: 10 MINUTES

This guacamole brings heat and a touch of sweetness from the roasted jalapeño, a pop of sourness from the lime, and the wonderful creamy texture and unique flavor of a ripe avocado.

1 to 3 jalapeños (depending on your preferred level of spiciness)
1 avocado, peeled and pitted
1 tablespoon freshly squeezed lime juice

1. Preheat the oven to 400°F. Line a baking sheet with parchment paper.
2. Place the jalapeños on the baking sheet and roast for 8 minutes. (The jalapeño can also be roasted on a grill for 5 minutes, if you already have it fired up.)
3. Slice the jalapeños down the center, and remove the seeds. Then cut the top stem off, and dice into ⅛-inch pieces. Wash your hands immediately after handling the jalapeños.
4. In a medium bowl, use a fork to mash together the avocado, jalapeño pieces, and lime juice. Continue mashing and mixing until the guacamole reaches your preferred consistency, and serve.

VARIATION TIP: A fun way to change up the guacamole or lessen the amount of fat per serving is to blend 1 cup steamed sweet peas into a smooth purée, then mix the peas in with the guacamole for a spicy-sweet pea guacamole.

PER SERVING
Calories: 77; Total fat: 7g; Carbohydrates: 5g; Fiber: 3g; Protein: 1g

White Bean and Chickpea Hummus

MAKES 3 CUPS

5 INGREDIENTS, 30 MINUTES, GLUTEN FREE, NUT FREE • PREP TIME: 5 MINUTES

Hummus has become almost synonymous with eating a vegan or plant-based diet. But currently, many of the store-bought options are filled with oil and salt. This recipe makes a tasty hummus that can be spread on a **Whole-Wheat Pita Pocket** or used as a delicious dip for vegetables. You can cook your own beans for this recipe, but canned beans work just fine.

1 (15-ounce) can chickpeas
1 (15-ounce) can white beans (cannellini or great northern)
3 tablespoons freshly squeezed lemon juice
2 teaspoons garlic powder
1 teaspoon onion powder

1. Drain and rinse the chickpeas and white beans.
2. In a food processor or blender, combine the chickpeas, beans, lemon juice, garlic powder, and onion powder. Process for 1 to 2 minutes, or until the texture is smooth and creamy.
3. Serve right away, or store in a refrigerator-safe container for up to 5 days.

VARIATION TIP: Add 1 teaspoon chili powder and ½ teaspoon cumin to create a Mexican-inspired hummus. Or toss in 1 teaspoon smoked paprika and 1 tablespoon maple syrup for a sweet and smoky hummus.

PER SERVING (¼ CUP)
Calories: 69; Total fat: 1g; Carbohydrates: 12g; Fiber: 4g; Protein: 4g

the dirty dozen™ and the clean fifteen™

The **Dirty Dozen™** are foods that have high levels of pesticide residues when conventionally grown. In 2019, the Environmental Working Group recommended buying the organic versions of the following whenever possible:

- Strawberries
- Spinach
- Kale
- Nectarines
- Apples
- Grapes
- Peaches
- Cherries
- Pears
- Tomatoes
- Celery
- Potatoes

The **Clean Fifteen™** were found to have the lowest amounts of pesticide contamination in 2019 and are considered safe to buy conventionally grown (nonorganic):

- Avocados
- Sweet Corn
- Pineapples
- Sweet Peas (Frozen)
- Onions

- Papayas
- Eggplants
- Asparagus
- Kiwis
- Cabbages
- Cauliflower
- Cantaloupes
- Broccoli
- Mushrooms
- Honeydew Melons

Measurement Conversions

VOLUME EQUIVALENTS (LIQUID)

US STANDARD	US STANDARD (OUNCES)	METRIC (APPROXIMATE)
2 tablespoons	1 fl. oz.	30 mL
¼ cup	2 fl. oz.	60 mL
½ cup	4 fl. oz.	120 mL
1 cup	8 fl. oz.	240 mL
1½ cups	12 fl. oz.	355 mL
2 cups or 1 pint	16 fl. oz.	475 mL
4 cups or 1 quart	32 fl. oz.	1 L
1 gallon	128 fl. oz.	4 L

OVEN TEMPERATURES

FAHRENHEIT	CELSIUS (APPROXIMATE)
250°F	120°C
300°F	150°C
325°F	165°C
350°F	180°C
375°F	190°C
400°F	200°C
425°F	220°C
450°F	230°C

VOLUME EQUIVALENTS (DRY)

US STANDARD	METRIC (APPROXIMATE)
⅛ teaspoon	0.5 mL
¼ teaspoon	1 mL
½ teaspoon	2 mL
¾ teaspoon	4 mL
1 teaspoon	5 mL
1 tablespoon	15 mL
¼ cup	59 mL
⅓ cup	79 mL
½ cup	118 mL
⅔ cup	156 mL
¾ cup	177 mL
1 cup	235 mL
2 cups or 1 pint	475 mL
3 cups	700 mL
4 cups or 1 quart	1 L

WEIGHT EQUIVALENTS

US STANDARD	METRIC (APPROXIMATE)
½ ounce	15 g
1 ounce	30 g
2 ounces	60 g
4 ounces	115 g
8 ounces	225 g
12 ounces	340 g
16 ounces or 1 pound	455 g

Resources

DOCUMENTARIES

PlantPure Nation by Nelson Campbell

Forks Over Knives by Lee Fulkerson

Eating You Alive by Paul David Kennamer Jr.

BOOKS

The Cheese Trap: How Breaking a Surprising Addiction Will Help You Lose Weight, Gain Energy, and Get Healthy by Neal Barnard

The China Study: The Most Comprehensive Study of Nutrition Ever Conducted and the Startling Implications for Diet, Weight Loss and Long-Term Health by T. Colin Campbell and Thomas M. Campbell

Prevent and Reverse Heart Disease: The Revolutionary, Scientifically Proven, Nutrition-Based Cure by Caldwell B. Esselstyn Jr.

How Not to Die: Discover the Foods Scientifically Proven to Prevent and Reverse Disease by Gene Stone and Michael Greger

The Healthiest Diet on the Planet: Why the Foods You Love—Pizza, Pancakes, Potatoes, Pasta, and More—Are the Solution to Preventing Disease and Looking and Feeling Your Best by John McDougall

The Alzheimer's Solution: A Breakthrough Program to Prevent and Reverse the Symptoms of Cognitive Decline at Every Age by Dean and Ayesha Sherzai

WEBSITES

ForksOverKnives.com

BrandNewVegan.com

PlantBasedGabriel.com

References

Abdulla, M., I. Andersson, N. G. Asp, K. Berthelsen, D. Birkhed, I. Dencker, C. G. Johansson, et al. "Nutrient Intake and Health Status of Vegans. Chemical Analyses of Diets Using the Duplicate Portion Sampling Technique." Abstract. *The American Journal of Clinical Nutrition* 34, no. 11 (November 1981): 2464–77. doi:10.1093/ajcn/34.11.2464.

Ahuja, Jaspreet K. C., Pamela R. Pehrsson, David B. Haytowitz, Shirley Wasswa-Kintu, Melissa Nickle, Bethany Showell, Robin Thomas, et al. "Sodium Monitoring in Commercially Processed and Restaurant Foods," *The American Journal of Clinical Nutrition* 101, no. 3 (March 2015): 622–31. doi:10.3945/ajcn.114.084954.

Albarracín, William, Iván C. Sánchez, Raúl Grau, and José M. Barat. "Salt in Food Processing; Usage and Reduction: A Review." Abstract. *International Journal of Food Science and Technology* 46, no. 7 (February 2, 2011): 1329–36. doi:10.1111/j.1365-2621.2010.02492.x.

Anderson, James W., Pat Baird, Richard H. Davis, Jr., Stefanie Ferreri, Mary Knudtson, Ashraf Koraym, Valerie Waters, and Christine L. Williams. "Health Benefits of Dietary Fiber." Abstract. *Nutrition Reviews* 67, no. 4 (April 2009): 188–205. doi:10.1111/j.1753-4887.2009.00189.x.

Balakumar, Pitchai, Khin Maung-U, and Gowraganahalli Jagadeesh. "Prevalence and Prevention of Cardiovascular Disease and Diabetes Mellitus." Abstract. *Pharmacological Research* 113, pt. A (November 2016): 600–09. doi:10.1016/j.phrs.2016.09.040.

Barnard, Neal D., Anthony R. Scialli, Gabrielle Turner-McGrievy, Amy J. Lanou, and Jolie Glass. "The Effects of a Low-Fat, Plant-Based Dietary Intervention on Body Weight, Metabolism, and Insulin Sensitivity," *The American Journal of Medicine* 118, no. 9 (September 2005): 991–97. doi:10.1016/j.amjmed.2005.03.039.

Barnard, Neal D., Heather I. Katcher, David J. A. Jenkins, Joshua Cohen, and Gabrielle Turner-McGrievy. "Vegetarian and Vegan Diets in Type 2 Diabetes Management." Abstract. *Nutrition Reviews* 67, no. 5 (May 2009): 255–63. doi:10.1111/j.1753-4887.2009.00198.x.

Barnard, Neal D., Joshua Cohen, David J. A. Jenkins, Gabrielle Turner-McGrievy, Lise Gloede, Brent Jaster, Kim Seidl, Amber A. Green, and Stanley Talpers. "A Low-Fat Vegan Diet Improves Glycemic Control and Cardiovascular Risk Factors in a Randomized Clinical Trial in Individuals with Type 2 Diabetes," *Diabetes Care* 29, no. 8 (August 2006): 1777–83. doi:10.2337/dc06-0606.

Beecher, Gary R. "Phytonutrients' Role in Metabolism: Effects on Resistance to Degenerative Processes." Abstract. *Nutrition Reviews* 57, no. 9 (September 1999): 3–6. doi:10.1111/j.1753-4887.1999.tb01800.x.

Boutayeb, Abdesslam, and Saber Boutayeb. "The Burden of Non Communicable Diseases in Developing Countries," *International Journal for Equity in Health* 4 no. 2 (2005). doi:10.1186/1475-9276-4-2.

Brown, C. M., A. G. Dulloo, and J-P. Montani. "Sugary Drinks in the Pathogenesis of Obesity and Cardiovascular Diseases," *International Journal of Obesity* 32 (2008): S28–S34. doi:10.1038/ijo.2008.204.

Buettner, Dan. *The Blue Zones: 9 Lessons for Living Longer from the People Who've Lived the Longest.* 2nd. ed. Washington, D.C.: National Geographic Society, 2012.

Campbell, T. Colin, Banoo Parpia, and Junshi Chen. "Diet, Lifestyle, and the Etiology of Coronary Artery Disease: The Cornell China Study," *The American Journal of Cardiology* 82, no. 10, sup. 2 (November 1998): 18– 21. doi:10.1016/S0002-9149(98)00718-8.

Cassidy, Emily S., Paul C. West, James S. Gerber, and Jonathan A. Foley. "Redefining Agricultural Yields: From Tonnes to People Nourished Per Hectare," *Environmental Research Letters* 8, no. 3 (August 2013): 1–8. doi:10.1088/1748-9326/8/3/034015.

Craig, Winston J. "Health Effects of Vegan Diets," *The American Journal of Clinical Nutrition* 89, no. 5 (May 2009): 1627S–33S. doi:10.3945/ajcn.2009.26736N.

Dawkins, Marian. "Welfare and the Structure of a Battery Cage: Size and Cage Floor Preferences in Domestic Hens." Abstract. *British Veterinary Journal* 134, no. 5 (September/October 1978): 469–75. doi:10.1016/S0007-1935(17)33389-4.

D'Elia, Lanfranco, Giovanni Rossi, Renato Ippolito, Francesco P. Cappuccio, and Pasquale Strazzullo. "Habitual Salt Intake and Risk of Gastric Cancer: A Meta-Analysis of Prospective Studies." Abstract. *Clinical Nutrition* 31, no. 4 (August 2012): 489–98. doi:10.1016/j.clnu.2012.01.003.

De Natale, Claudia, Giovanni Annuzzi, Lutgarda Bozzetto, Raffaella Mazzarella, Giuseppina Costabile, Ornella Ciano, Gabriele Riccardi, and Angela A. Rivellese. "Effects of a Plant-Based High-Carbohydrate/High-Fiber Diet Versus High-Monounsaturated Fat/Low-Carbohydrate Diet on Postprandial Lipids in Type 2 Diabetic Patients," *Diabetes Care* 32, no. 12 (December 2009): 2168–73. doi:10.2337/dc09-0266.

Dickinson, Kacie M., Jennifer B. Keogh, and Peter M. Clifton. "Effects of a Low-Salt Diet on Flow-Mediated Dilatation in Humans," *The American Journal of Clinical Nutrition* 89, no. 2 (February 2009): 485–90. doi:10.3945/ajcn.2008.26856.

Environmental Protection Agency. "Global Greenhouse Gas Emissions Data." https://www.epa.gov/ghgemissions/global-greenhouse-gas-emissions-data .

Esselstyn, Caldwell B. "A Plant-Based Diet and Coronary Artery Disease: A Mandate for Effective Therapy," in "A Plant-Based Diet and Cardiovascular Disease," *Journal of Geriatric Cardiology* 14, no. 5 (May 2017): 317–20. doi:10.11909/j.issn.1671-5411.2017.05.004.

Frances, Heather M., and Richard J. Stevenson. "Higher Reported Saturated Fat and Refined Sugar Intake Is Associated with Reduced Hippocampal-

Dependent Memory and Sensitivity to Interoceptive Signals." Abstract. *Behavioral Neuroscience* 125, no. 6 (December 2011): 943–55. doi:10.1037/a0025998.

Fraser, Gary, and David Shavlik. "Ten Years of Life: Is It a Matter of Choice?" *Archives of Internal Medicine* 161, no. 13 (July 2001): 1645–52. doi:10.1001/archinte.161.13.1645.

Fuhrman, Joel, and Deana M. Ferreri. "Fueling the Vegetarian (Vegan) Athlete," *Current Sports Medicine Reports* 9, no. 4 (July/August 2010): 233–41. doi:10.1249/JSR.0b013e3181e93a6f.

Fukagawa, N. K., J. W. Anderson, G. Hageman, V. R. Young, and K. L. Minaker. "High Carbohydrate, High-Fiber Diets Increase Peripheral Insulin Sensitivity in Healthy Young and Old Adults." Abstract. *The American Journal of Clinical Nutrition* 52, no. 3 (September 1990): 524–28. doi:10.1093/ajcn/52.3.524.

Giem, P., W. L. Beeson, and G. E. Fraser. "The Incidence of Dementia and the Intake of Animal Products: Preliminary Findings from the Adventist Health Study." Abstract. *Neuro-epidemiology* 12 (1993): 28–36. doi:10.1159/000110296.

Gillespie, Cathleen, Joyce Maalouf, Keming Yuan, Mary E. Cogswell, Janelle P. Gunn, Jessica Levings, Alanna Moshfegh, Jaspreet K. C. Ahuja, and Robert Merritt. "Sodium Content in Major Brands of US Packaged Foods, 2009," *The American Journal of Clinical Nutrition* 101, no. 2 (February 2015): 344–53. doi:10.3945/ajcn.113.078980.

Harvard Medical School. "Meat or Beans: What Will You Have? Part 1: Meat." Harvard Health Publishing. Published February 2011. https://www.health.harvard.edu/staying-healthy/meat-or-beans-what-will-you-have-part-i-meat .

Heron, Melonie, and Robert N. Anderson. "Changes in the Leading Cause of Death: Recent Patterns in Heart Disease and Cancer Mortality." NCHS Data Brief No. 254. National Center for Health Statistics, Centers for

Disease Control and Prevention. August 2016. https://www.cdc.gov/nchs/products/databriefs/db254.htm .

Institute of Medicine. "Chapter 9: Vitamin B12." In *Dietary Reference Intakes for Thiamin, Riboflavin, Niacin, Vitamin B6, Folate, Vitamin B12, Pantothenic Acid, Biotin, and Choline,* 306–56. Washington, D.C.: The National Academies Press, 1998. doi:10.17226/6015.

Jaksch, Walter. "Euthanasia of Day-Old Male Chicks in the Poultry Industry," *International Journal for the Study of Animal Problems* 2, no. 4 (1981): 203–13. https://animalstudiesrepository.org/cgi/viewcontent.cgi?referer=https://scholar.google.com/&httpsredir=1&article=1024&context=acwp_faafp .

Kahleova, Hana, Susan Levin, and Neal Barnard. "Cardio-Metabolic Benefits of Plant-Based Diets," in "The Science of Vegetarian Nutrition and Health," ed. Karen Jaceldo-Siegl, special issue, *Nutrients* 9, no. 8 (2017): 848. doi:10.3390/nu9080848.

Le, Lap Tai, and Joan Sabaté. "Beyond Meatless, the Health Effects of Vegan Diets: Findings from the Adventist Cohorts," *Nutrients* 6, no. 6 (2014): 2131–47. doi:10.3390/nu6062131.

Liu, Rui Hai. "Health Benefits of Fruits and Vegetables Are from Additive and Synergistic Combinations of Phytochemicals," *The American Journal of Clinical Nutrition* 78, no. 3 (September 2003): 517S-520S. doi:10.1093/ajcn/78.3.517S.

Lobstein, T., L. Baur, and R. Uauy. "Obesity in Children and Young People: A Crisis in Public Health," *Obesity Reviews* 5, sup. 1 (April 2004): 4–85. doi:10.1111/j.1467-789X.2004.00133.x.

McCarty, M. F. "Vegan Proteins May Reduce Risk of Cancer, Obesity, and Cardiovascular Disease by Promoting Increased Glucagon Activity," *Medical Hypotheses* 53, no. 6 (December 1999): 459–85. doi:10.1054/mehy.1999.0784.

McDougall, John, Laurie E. Thomas, Craig McDougall, Gavin Moloney, Bradley Saul, John S. Finnell, Kelly Richardson, and Katelin Mae Peterson. "Effects of 7 Days on an Ad Libitum Low-Fat Vegan Diet: The McDougall Program Cohort," *Nutrition Journal* 13, no. 99 (2014). doi:10.1186/1475-2891-13-99.

McMacken, Michelle, and Sapana Shah. "A Plant-Based Diet for the Prevention and Treatment of Type 2 Diabetes," *Journal of Geriatric Cardiology* 14, no. 5 (May 2017): 342–54. doi:10.11909/j.issn.1671-5411.2017.05.009.

Mokdad, Ali H., Barbara A. Bowman, Earl S. Ford, Frank Vinicor, James S. Marks, and Jeffrey P. Koplan. "The Continuing Epidemics of Obesity and Diabetes in the United States," *JAMA* 286, no. 10 (2001): 1195–1200. doi:10.1001/jama.286. 10.1195.

Molteni, Raffaella, R. James Barnard, Zhe Ying, Christian K. Roberts, and Fernando Gómez-Pinilla. "A High-Fat, Refined Sugar Diet Reduces Hippocampal Brain-Derived Neurotrophic Factor, Neuronal Plasticity, and Learning." Abstract. *Neuroscience* 112, no. 4 (July 2002): 803–14. doi:10.1016/S0306-4522(02)00123-9.

Moore, Wendy J., Michael E. McGrievy, Gabrielle M. Turner-McGrievy. "Dietary Adherence and Acceptability of Five Different Diets, Including Vegan and Vegetarian Diets, for Weight Loss: A New DIETs Study." Abstract. *Eating Behaviors* 19 (December 2015): 33–38. doi:10.1016/j.eatbeh.2015.06.011.

Neustadt, John. "The Food Pyramid and Disease Prevention," *Integrative Medicine* 4, no. 6 (December 2005/January 2006): 14–9. https://nbihealth.com/wp-content/uploads/2017/10/Neustadt-Food-Pyramid-Article.pdf .

O'Connell, M. K., P. B. Lynch, S. Bertholot, F. Verlait, and P. G. Lawlor. "Measuring Changes in Physical Size and Predicting Weight of Sows During Gestation," *Animal* 1, no. 9 (October 2007): 1335–43. doi:10.1017/S1751731107000559.

Ogden, Cynthia L., Margaret D. Carroll, Brian K. Kit, and Katherine M. Flegal. "Prevalence of Childhood and Adult Obesity in the United States, 2011–2012," *JAMA* 311, no. 8 (2014): 806–814. doi:10.1001/jama.2014.732.

O'Neil, Carol E., Debra R. Keast, Victor L. Fulgoni, and Theresa A. Nicklas. "Food Sources of Energy and Nutrients among Adults in the US: NHANES 2003–2006." *Nutrients* 4, no. 12 (2012): 2097–120. doi:10.3390/nu4122097.

Orlich, Michael J., Pramil N. Singh, Joan Sabaté, Karen Jaceldo-Siegl, Jing Fan, Synnove Knutsen, W. Lawrence Beeson, and Gary E. Fraser. "Vegetarian Dietary Patterns and Mortality in Adventist Health Study 2," *JAMA Internal Medicine* 173, no. 13 (2013): 1230–38. doi:10.1001/jamainternmed.2013.6473.

Phillips, Katherine M., Monica H. Carlsen, and Rune Blomhoff. "Total Antioxidant Content of Alternatives to Refined Sugar." Abstract. *Journal of the Academy of Nutrition and Dietetics* 109, no. 1 (January 2009): 64–71. doi:10.1016/j.jada.2008.10.014.

Rueda-Clausen, Christian F., Federico A. Silva, Manuel A. Lindarte, Cristina Villa-Roel, Elieth Gomez, Roberto Gutierrez, Carlos Cure-Cure, and Patricio López-Jaramillo. "Olive, Soybean and Palm Oils Have a Similar Acute Detrimental Effect over the Endothelial Function in Healthy Young Subjects," *Nutrition, Metabolism & Cardiovascular Diseases* 17, no. 1 (January 2007): 50–57. doi:10.1016/j.numecd.2005.08.008.

Sabaté, Joan, and Sam Soret. "Sustainability of Plant-Based Diets: Back to the Future," *The American Journal of Clinical Nutrition* 100, sup. 1 (July 2014): 476S–482S. doi:10.3945/ajcn.113.071522.

Scarborough, Peter, Paul N. Appleby, Anja Mizdrak, Adam D. M. Briggs, Ruth C. Travis, Kathryn E. Bradbury, and Timothy J. Key. "Dietary Greenhouse Gas Emissions of Meat-Eaters, Fish-Eaters, Vegetarians and Vegans in the UK," *Climatic Change* 125, no. 2 (July 2014): 179–92. doi:10.1007/s10584-014-1169-1.

Scott D. C. B., and J.F. Muir. "Offshore Cage Systems: A Practical Overview," in "Mediterranean Offshore Mariculture" *Options Méditerranéennes: Série B. Etudes et Recherches*, no. 30 (2000): 79–89. http://om.iamm.fr/om/pdf/b30/00600651.pdf .

Snowdon, David A., Roland L. Phillips, and Gary E. Fraser. "Meat Consumption and Fatal Ischemic Heart Disease." Abstract. *Preventive Medicine* 13, no. 5 (1984): 490–500. doi:10.1016/0091-7435(84)90017-3.

Song, Mingyang, Teresa T. Fung, Frank B. Hu, Walter C. Willett, Valter D. Longo, Andrew T. Chan, and Edward L. Giovannucci. "Association of Animal and Plant Protein Intake with All-Cause and Cause-Specific Mortality," *JAMA Internal Medicine* 176, no. 10 (2016): 1453–63. doi:10.1001/jamainternmed.2016.4182.

Steinfeld, Henning, Pierre Gerber, Tom Wassenaar, Vincent Castel, Mauricio Rosales, and Cees de Haan. *Livestock's Long Shadow: Environmental Issues and Options.* Rome: Food and Agriculture Organization of the United Nations, 2006. http://www.fao.org/3/a0701e/a0701e00.htm .

Thomas, Art and Ron Garland. "Supermarket Shopping Lists: Their Effect on Consumer Expenditure." Abstract. *International Journal of Retail & Distribution Management* 21, no. 2 (1993). doi:10.1108/09590559310028040.

Tobian, Louis J. "The Relationship of Salt to Hypertension." Abstract. *The American Journal of Clinical Nutrition* 32, no. 12 (1979): 2739–48. http://agris.fao.org/agris-search/search.do?recordID=US8020211 .

Trafton, Anne. "MIT Biologists Solve Vitamin Puzzle," MIT News. Updated March 21, 2007. http://news.mit.edu/2007/b12 .

Troutt, H. F., and B. I. Osburn. "Meat from Dairy Cows: Possible Microbiological Hazards and Risks," *Scientific and Technical Review of the Office International des Epizooties* 16, no. 2 (1997): 405–14. https://pdfs.semanticscholar.org/163b/d2c5372ded7fc2db3cc1483be71ae588adca.pdf .

Tucker, K. L., S. Rich, I. Rosenberg, P. Jacques, G. Dallal, P. W. F. Wilson, and J. Selhub. "Plasma Vitamin B-12 Concentrations Relate to Intake Source in the Framingham Offspring Study," *The American Journal of Clinical Nutrition* 71, no. 2 (February 2000): 514–22. doi:10.1093/ajcn/71.2.514.

Turner-McGrievy, Gabrielle, Trisha Mandes, and Anthony Crimarco. "A Plant-Based Diet for Overweight and Obesity Prevention and Treatment," *Journal of Geriatric Cardiology* 14, no. 5 (May 2017): 369–74. doi:10.11909/j.issn.1671-5411.2017.05.002.

Tuso, Phillip J., Mohamed H. Ismail, Benjamin P. Ha, and Carole Bartolotto. "Nutritional Update for Physicians: Plant-Based Diets," *The Permanente Journal* 17, no. 2 (Spring 2013): 61–66. doi:10.7812/TPP/12-085.

United States Department of Agriculture, Economic Research Service. "Livestock, Dairy, and Poultry Outlook." LDP-M-282. Washington, D.C.: United States Department of Agriculture. 2018. https://www.ers.usda.gov/webdocs/publications/86243/ldp-m-282.pdf?v=0 .

Vang, A., P. N. Singh, J. W. Lee, E. H. Haddad, and C. H. Brinegar. "Meats, Processed Meats, Obesity, Weight Gain and Occurrence of Diabetes among Adults: Findings from Adventist Health Studies." Abstract. *Annals of Nutrition & Metabolism* 52 (2008): 96–104. doi:10.1159/000121365.

Walter, Paul. "Effects of Vegetarian Diets on Aging and Longevity," *Nutrition Reviews* 55, no. 1 (January 1997): S61-S65. http://doc.rero.ch/record/293972/files/nutritionreviews55-s061.pdf .

Weinberger, M. H. "Salt Sensitivity of Blood Pressure in Humans," *Hypertension* 27, no. 3 (March 1996): 481–90. doi:10.1161/01.HYP.27.3.481.

Wilcox, D. Craig, Bradley J. Wilcox, Hidemi Todoriki, and Makoto Suzuki. "The Okinawan Diet: Health Implications of a Low-Calorie, Nutrient-Dense, Antioxidant-Rich Dietary Pattern Low in Glycemic Load," *Journal of the American College of Nutrition* 28, sup. 4 (2009): 500S–516S. doi:10.1080/07315724.2009.10718117.